Finding Your Soul

Don Durrett

Copyright © 2011 Don Durrett
All Rights Reserved
(Third Edition July 2012)

No part of this book may be reproduced in any form or by any electronic or mechanical means including information storage and retrieval systems, without permission in writing from the author.

ISBN: 978-1-4276-5190-7

www.dondurrett.com

Books by Don Durrett

Last of the Gnostics

A Stranger From the Past

Conversations With an Immortal

Spirit Club

New Thinking for the New Age

Finding Your Soul

Finding Your Soul Workbook

Love yourself with purity and respect.
Love others with compassion and gentleness.
Love God with honor and truth.

Trust that your life was pre-planned.
Trust that life is divinely ordered.
Trust that nothing can happen to you
that is not supposed to.

– Don Durrett

Contents

Introduction iii
Foreword vii
Chapter One
   Ireland 1
Chapter Two
   Back to School 27
Chapter Three
   Know Your Self 35
Chapter Four
   Jenny and Ted 43
Chapter Five
   The Announcement 53
Chapter Six
   Reincarnation 65
Chapter Seven
   Santa Fe 81
Chapter Eight
   New Age Convention 93
Chapter Nine
   Dan 103
Chapter Ten
   Washington 119
Chapter 11
   Ogmios 135
Chapter Twelve
   Finding Your Soul 153
EPILOGUE 175

Introduction

When I began writing metaphysical books, I had one goal in mind: I wanted to expose people to what I had learned. I wanted to expand the reader's awareness as my awareness had been expanded. I have learned that awareness is the most fundamental aspect of life. Awareness is the understanding of who we are and what life is about.

Awareness can be expanded by learning about metaphysics (beyond the physical). With this knowledge, you no longer have to live with a narrow view of reality. Instead, you can have a much broader view of who you are and what life is about. This book is about exposing you to that broader view. If this is your first exposure to metaphysical concepts, you should find this material fascinating.

Metaphysical knowledge is real and will make you think about life from a new perspective. Many of your current beliefs will be exposed as false, and this will force you to reconsider what you believe. Metaphysical knowledge can change the way you think, and thus your life. It is literally the truth that can set you free.

I have used a story based in the near future to explain metaphysical concepts. Although the story provides an entertaining background, I use it to convey concepts. I am not sure if all of the concepts in this book are 100% correct. At this time, I believe them to be, but only time will tell.

The concepts in this book are my truths. For this reason, I suggest that you find correlating data before you accept these ideas as your own. I do not think you can find your truth using just one source. That is what spirituality is all about — finding *your* truth.

I based the plot of this book on a prophecy from Nostradamus. At one time, his prediction of a world war led by an Arab antichrist was a possible future. Thank goodness, it did not transpire, leaving this book a fictional story that will not actually happen. The prediction was as follows: the so-called antichrist rises to power in the Middle East; the world economy collapses; the antichrist cajoles the world into accepting him as a legitimate, peaceful world leader; then the antichrist starts his world war to conquer the world.

The purpose of all my books is to help people understand and prepare for the coming changes to civilization. Although we are not going to have a world war, the one overriding theme I use in all of my books is the imminent end of our current civilization. I believe 100% that we are at the cusp of a transition into a *new* civilization. And this is not going to happen in the distant future, but during our lifetimes.

The basis of this transition is spiritual in nature. Civilization is going to literally transform spiritually. Instead of a civilization that is fragmented by an array of different cultures, countries, and religions, we are going to come together as a global community based on spirituality and human values. This will occur as people recognize the inherent divinity that we each hold and the inherent *oneness* of life, or how we are all part of the same whole.

How could this happen? How could people believe in the *oneness* of life? Well, many people already do, and this number is increasing every day. Steadily, we are progressing spiritually to the point where it will be common knowledge and accepted across the globe.

This vision may seem far-fetched, but the inevitability of this outcome will become apparent very soon. My estimate is sometime between 2016 and 2018. Once we become aware of our divinity, everything will change. Our world will become a love-

Introduction

based civilization instead of a power-based one. We are going to get along with each other, and love will reign. So, no matter how bad it appears to get over the next few years, the outcome will be wonderful. However, before you get giddy with excitement, the transition period will be quite tumultuous, and many will perish. For those fortunate enough to survive the chaotic transition period from 2012 to approximately 2035, the future will be everything we want it to be and more: a utopian paradise.

So now you know why I write the books that I write. I want to help people prepare for this coming new world. And because the foundation will be a new spiritual philosophy, that is the basis of my writings. Although I most likely do not have it completely right, I am close. Moreover, by reading this material, you will be much more prepared for the future than the average person who has had no exposure to metaphysics.

Foreword

I remember last year well. For me, it began in Ireland. I had been asked to go to Europe to talk with the Underground about the New Age movement. At the time, I had no idea that this would be the first in a series of unexpected events...

CHAPTER ONE

Ireland

I walked along a path next to a short stone wall. Everywhere I looked, there was bright green grass and low stone walls to keep in the sheep. I constantly glanced at the beautiful, green rolling hills off in the distance. It was stunning. I was on my way to a pub to meet with several members of the Underground. It was chilly out, and the wind was gusting. My jacket was barely keeping me warm.

I was in a small village just outside Dublin. I had arrived yesterday via a 747 from Los Angeles. I had come as a favor to friends of mine in the New Age movement. There had been a request from the Underground for a meeting with a New Age leader.

In no way was I a New Age leader. I was anything but. I led a very low-profile lifestyle. I was a teacher. I taught metaphysical knowledge at an obscure, tiny school in California. Many New Age leaders, however, were my friends.

It was my friendship with these leaders that had sent me twelve hours across the Atlantic. I had agreed to come, but not as a member of any organization. This was not the beginning of my association with the leadership. In many respects, I don't know why I had agreed to come. It didn't fit my normal behavior.

I found the pub and entered. Darkness. I sat down on a bar stool and waited for the bartender. The few people at the bar paid no particular attention to me. A fire burned in the fireplace, and it was cozy and warm. A calico cat was curled up asleep near the fire.

It was an old pub. The walls were made of wood and smelled of rot from decades of decay. I glanced at the numerous kegs of beer aligned behind the bar. I searched for Samuel Smith's, but it was not to be found.

"What will it be, lad?" the bartender asked.

"Water will be fine, thank you," I replied.

When he heard my accent, his demeanor changed. He squinted his eyes and looked me over carefully.

"Are ye looking for Jimmy, then?" he asked.

I nodded.

"This way, lad," he said.

He turned and walked down the hall to the back of the bar. I followed. He opened a door to a back room and ushered me in. There, in front of me, were four men sitting around a table, drinking beer and smoking cigarettes.

"Here's your visitor, Jimmy."

"Thanks, Danny," Jimmy replied.

Danny, the bartender, closed the door on his way out. I looked at the four gentlemen. They were all dressed in local working man clothes, but they were not all locals. Who were these guys? And what did they really want?

I had been pondering these questions for the last two weeks. The New Age leaders didn't know. They told me that a request had come from the Underground in Europe for information regarding the New Age movement in America. The Underground had requested someone to come and explain what the movement was about.

Chapter 1 - Ireland

Jimmy rose from his chair and came around the table to meet me. He extended his hand and gave me a warm smile. I had the impression that he was a local Irishman.

"It's a pleasure to meet you, John," he said, in his deep Irish accent.

The others were quickly on their feet, extending their hands. I shook each, in turn. They all had strong grips and intensity in their eyes. Jimmy, however, was the only one with enthusiasm. The others were more reserved. I noticed quickly that only Jimmy was Irish. The others were European—and tough looking. Most likely, they were soldiers in the Underground.

"Have a seat, John," Jimmy said. "We have a lot to talk about. Would you like a beer?"

"Water would be good," I said.

"Okay, I'll be right back," Jimmy said, as he left the room.

I glanced at the three Europeans. What did these men want? There was silence as we found our respective chairs. One of the Europeans turned on a tape recorder. The room was nondescript, with bare wooden walls and a single light overhead. The floor was dirty cement, although recently swept. I had the impression that this room was usually a place to play cards.

We waited for Jimmy to return. He came back and placed a glass of ice water in front of me. "Thank you," I said.

One of the Europeans began talking. "You're here because you were specifically requested by the leader of the Underground."

I was taken aback, as this was news to me. I had not been told that I had been specifically requested. It made me wonder what other information was liable to pop up next.

"One of your students volunteered into the Underground, a few years ago," he continued. "We call him New Ager. He tries to teach others your New Age principles: that we are *all* eternal; that this life is just another experience added to our soul; that God loves *all* equally; and on."

"He never stops talking," added one of the other Europeans, sardonically.

We all laughed, and the tension in the room was suddenly gone.

"The leader wants to hear your opinions. What is this war about? What is the meaning of it? The war has been going on for seven years now and it is stalemated. Europe is turning into an eternal battlefield, as the AC encroaches upon every free nation on earth." The military leader he was referring to was usually referred to as the antichrist, or the AC, for short.

"Our leader is also curious about the impact the New Age movement is having on the world. How strong is it in America? Is it going to be exported to the rest of the world?" He finished and waited for my reply.

I paused in contemplation, as I reflected upon the running tape recorder. "So, we have this conversation, and it's recorded for the leader? Then what?"

The same European who had been speaking shrugged. "Who knows? We're just following orders. I like New Ager, and I talk to him a lot, as does the leader. We want to find out more."

The other Europeans smoked their cigarettes and remained quiet.

"What's your name?" I asked the European who had been doing the talking.

"Renan."

"Nice to meet you, Renan. Okay, let's talk. I came a long ways. I might as well answer your questions."

"Tell us about New Age spirituality," he said, taking a drink from his pint of Guinness.

Chapter 1 - Ireland

I nodded. "Now, some of what you hear today may make little sense. It might sound bizarre, strange, and quite unbelievable. But, before I begin, I want you to understand that I'm not making this up. Knowledge has been released that explains the answers to all of the questions that have plagued humankind. Who are we? Why are we here? What is the meaning of life? I, as well as many others, possess this knowledge."

The seriousness in my voice got their attention. One of the quiet Europeans actually gasped.

Truth can be unsettling. As such, I try not to expose people to the truth who can't handle it. This was not such an occasion.

"So, you want to know about New Age spirituality? Okay, I'll tell you. The planet Earth and the other billions of planets in the universe reside on the physical plane. The physical plane is an illusion. It is nothing more than vibrating energy."

I pounded on the table for emphasis. "This is not a table. It is *energy*, vibrating to appear to be a table. The raw material of the physical plane is only one thing—energy. Everything is made of the same thing, but more than that, it is the consciousness of *God*. To repeat, *all* energy encompasses the consciousness of God."

"Are you saying that this table is God?" Renan asked, with a look of curiosity.

I nodded. "Not only is God this table, but the table is *alive*. God *is* the physical plane. God is you. God is me. But more than that, there is no separation between God and *anything*. God is absolute. God is all. Thus, *we* are God and so is the table. I repeat: *there is no separation* between God and anything."

"Whoa," Renan said. "Slow down. How can that be? How can God be *everything*?"

"Simple. God cannot create anything unless it is from God. Thus, all energy comes from God and is a part of God."

"Wow, that's fascinating, John," Jimmy said. "God is the one, all-knowing absolute."

I nodded. "Just like your body is aware of every cell in your body, God is aware of every cell in God's body."

"So," Jimmy said, "God's body encompasses everything?"

I nodded. "God is energy, but more than that, God is consciousness. God is a consciousness that pervades and interrelates and directs everything. Every atom, every molecule, is connected to God. Everything has God's consciousness and thus is impacted by God.

"God is the absolute, but is also constantly changing and evolving. There is only *one* source, and that is God. There is no duality with God. There is no counter-balance. God *is* perfection, and all of God's creations *are* perfection. You, me, *everything*, was created in perfection. We have no blemish. We are eternal. What we perceive to be imperfection is nothing more than an illusion. God does not play with dice. Everything is perfectly orchestrated."

"You say this with such confidence," Renan said. "How can you *know*?"

"As I said earlier, knowledge has been released over the last fifty or so years. The veil concealing the other side—the spiritual plane—has been lowered, and many people have been able to communicate with the other side. It began to proliferate in the 1960s, with Jane Roberts, and has continued to this day.

"Now, let's go back to my explanation. This planet was created by God to experience life as if anew. From these experiences on the physical plane, we have the opportunity to evolve as individual pieces of God. God does not need to evolve, but can. We provide that opportunity as individual aspects of God. That is the only reason for the physical plane to exist. All of our brothers and sisters currently here are experiencing, in order to evolve and grow spiritually. We do it in cooperation."

Jimmy joked irreverently, "There doesn't seem to be much cooperation with the antichrist!"

Everyone laughed with him.

"It may appear that way," I said. "But at the core level of our souls, we are all cooperating. We are all equals playing our roles. The differences that we perceive are only illusions. Underneath the façade is God."

"God is the antichrist?" Jimmy asked incredulously.

I nodded.

Renan looked into my eyes with a serious expression. "You mean there are no differences between the good guys and the bad guys?"

I took a drink of water. "Exactly. It's just God experiencing life. Everyone and everything you see is God. Not only that, but everything is connected. For this reason, there are no accidents, and everything is done in cooperation."

Renan grimaced, as if in pain, "Murder is done in cooperation?"

I nodded. "What happens to us in this lifetime happens only with our agreement and acceptance. Nothing happens by chance. Everything that can happen is planned beforehand. We know exactly what we are getting into, before we are even born. Like I said, God doesn't play with dice."

Renan let out a deep breath. "That's hard to accept."

"I know," I said. "That's why unconditional love is so rare on this planet."

No one replied, so I continued. "The complexity of our lives on the physical plane is staggering. There is nothing simple about it. Most people perceive that they are alone. Nothing could be further from the truth. No one is alone. We all have a higher self—the soul—who watches over us and directs us. We also have guides, often called *guardian angels*, who watch over us and direct us. And then there is God, the *controlling force* that watches out for everyone's interest."

"Does that mean God is directing the war?" Renan asked.

"God is involved, but so is our free choice. However, nothing happens by chance. Everything is decided by our choices, which are based on beliefs. Thus, the war didn't occur because of one man—the AC. That's not how it works. Everything is planned in advance on the spiritual plane. In fact, everything has already happened."

Jimmy winced at the concept, unsure if he could wrap his mind around it. "Already happened? How can *that* be?"

"How can it *not* be?" I replied. "Haven't you heard of people who have known the future? Nostradamus or Edgar Cayce? Or people who have dreams of events that then occur? How can people know the future if it hasn't already happened? That's how life is perfect, because everything has already happened. Life is just rewind or replay."

Jimmy ran his fingers through his long matted hair, contemplating the ramifications. He wasn't sure what to believe. "So, what about free choice?"

"There are many possible futures," I said. "We have free choice to decide which future to live. We can end this war tomorrow, if enough people tire of it."

They were silent on this point. "Before we incarnate, we are shown scenes of potential lives and the experiences we could have. We get to choose which life we want to lead. All of it is based on the fact that these lives have *already* occurred. You may ask, "How could this be?" If you think the movie *The Matrix* was interesting, multiply the imagination of the creator of *The Matrix* by a billion and you come close to the imagination of God. God

Chapter 1 - Ireland

imagined many, many scenarios for Earth. We are just playing some of those scenarios back."

I paused and took a drink of water. I scanned my guests to see if they were paying attention. Jimmy and Renan were intrigued and interested. The other two Europeans thought I was nuts.

I continued. "Think of the complexity of nature. How clouds form and create storms and how they disperse and create sunshine. The complexity of nature is controlled by the consciousness of God, and *so are we*. Everything is interrelated, and nothing is separate — and the controlling force is God.

"God is the source of everything, because it was God's imagination that created everything. There are no mistakes and no accidents, because, before it happens, it was already God's imagination. All outcomes have already been imagined, and only those outcomes can come to pass."

"Why would God imagine war? Why?" Renan pleaded. He had difficulty accepting this idea.

"To experience the infinite," I replied. "We see carnage that appears heinous to us. Logically, it appears absurd that God would imagine this, but God imagines both positive and negative experiences. God imagines and attempts to experience *all* possibilities. We are the means that allow God to experience. We are the eyes and ears. We experience what God has imagined."

"Are you saying," Renan said, "that life is like a video game. That it isn't real? That it doesn't matter what happens?"

"I'm going to throw up," Jimmy said. "How can God be so evil?"

I took another drink of water. "Evil is an illusion. It's simply the word *live* spelled backwards. Evil is living without harmony. As I've said, life is perfect. Why? Because it's already happened — it's an illusion. To God, all experience is an imagination, and God knows all the outcomes."

"This sounds like bollocks to me," Jimmy said defiantly.

I hesitated at his defiance, wondering if he had something else to say.

"I'm sorry," Jimmy said, suddenly embarrassed. "Keep talking; we're not here to argue with you. This tape's for the leader, not us."

"It's okay," I said. "I don't mind your feedback."

He nodded.

I continued. "We incarnate on the physical plane to play a role. Our roles have many variations and free choice allows us to choose among those variations. Within every role is the potential to choose positive or negative outcomes. We are all tested. We all have the option of choosing only positive experiences."

Jimmy beamed. "Oh, now I understand. God imagines negative experiences, but we don't have to choose them. We don't have to choose war."

I nodded and returned his smile. "Exactly. We have the choice to go either way, and God allows us to choose. When we live on the spiritual plane, everything is in harmony. We know who we are and we only choose positive experiences. We incarnate on the physical plane to experience something different and to evolve as aspects of God.

"Incarnating on physical planets allows us to experience the full array of emotions, something that is not possible on the spiritual plane. Some of these planets, such as Earth, provide extreme negativity, but this is not bad or evil. God desires to experience both the negative and the positive. Otherwise, it would not be."

"That kind of makes sense," Renan said. "How else can we learn, other than from our mistakes?"

I nodded. "And in heaven, we can't make mistakes. Most souls on this planet are lacking in spiritual awareness and make

Chapter 1 - Ireland

mistakes right and left. These mistakes add to their karma. Then, many more incarnations are required to attain enlightenment.

"Mature and old souls have incarnated many times and have achieved a degree of spiritual wisdom. This wisdom curtails their mistakes and allows them to have mostly positive experiences. However, this planet has mostly been conducive to young and immature souls who desire negative experiences. This is about to change, as those with spiritual wisdom begin to exert more influence."

"So, the New Age movement is going to stop the war?" Renan asked seriously.

I laughed. "Not quite. Let me try to help you understand the current state of evolution on this planet. This planet has had an interesting history. Before this civilization, there have been many others. For example, the civilization of Atlantis thrived thousands of years ago. They were actually more advanced than we are today and lived in peace and harmony for thousands of years. Then they destroyed themselves. Why? What happened?

"Civilizations always rise and fall. It is natural for civilizations to collapse. In fact, all civilizations eventually perish. Although, most do not perish turbulently, but instead, evolve in harmonious ways. For instance, the next civilization on this planet shall live in relative harmony for approximately six thousand years. However, even that civilization shall perish.

"Today we are experiencing the end of the current civilization. What happened to Atlantis is repeating. It all comes down to God's imagination, and God always imagines an ending. It just happens to be the time for the birth of a new civilization, and the new civilization will be based on New Age thought.

"Each planet and each civilization has its own, unique experiences. This planet's experiences have been very volatile, and the array of experiences has been diverse. Terra—the actual name of this planet—is widely respected on the spiritual plane for the experiences it provides.

"The majority of the people in America are either young souls or early-stage mature souls. People at this level have very little conception of the reality of *oneness*. They believe that each of us is alone and separate from God and that a capricious God determines our fates.

"What makes us young souls or old souls is our level of awareness. Eventually, we all become wise old souls. The average person on this planet has lived over a hundred lives on the physical plane, attempting to obtain spiritual wisdom. Many old souls, such as myself, have lived more than a thousand.

"In addition to our levels of awareness, the planet itself has a level of awareness. This is the reason the planet is about to begin a new civilization. In recent years, enough people have been born with high levels of awareness to create a change. Or, I should say, God imagined enough wise old souls to create a new civilization."

Renan asked. "Enough people are becoming spiritually aware to create a change?"

I nodded. "Yes, enough to create a revolution. Indeed, to create a new civilization based on love."

Jimmy's eyes widened. "Peace on Earth?"

I nodded. "Soon. During our lifetimes."

"Keep talking, then. I'm listening," Jimmy said, in his thick Irish accent.

"Our lives are determined by the planet's mass consciousness—our collective beliefs. Everyone who presently lives here on this planet contributes to it. It is our thoughts and our beliefs that make up this consciousness. Also, understand that this consciousness is dynamic—it is fluid. The interrelation between our consciousness and the planet's consciousness is complex and ongoing, yet ordered."

Chapter 1 - Ireland

"My God," Renan said with a sense of awe, "I'm actually starting to understand this. As more and more people become aware, they affect this mass consciousness. Then the mass consciousness creates new experiences based on what we ask for—from our beliefs and thoughts."

I smiled. "You're catching on. The current war that we find ourselves in is a natural result of the mass consciousness. It is not right or wrong. It simply is. It is the result of our collective beliefs. It is an experience that we have collectively selected. It is nothing more, and nothing less. There is no underlying meaning. Life simply is."

I stopped and took a sip of water.

"My God, lad, you're making sense," Jimmy said, somewhat rattled.

Renan unfolded a piece of paper. "We have some questions."

I nodded. "Okay."

He read from the sheet of paper. "Is the New Age movement having an impact on America?"

I nodded. "Very much so. It's having a huge impact. Metaphysics is increasingly becoming accepted by mainstream society, and more so every day. We have metaphysical healing centers across the nation, where many of the healers are children, and thousands of people go every day. The mass media and entertainment shows are littered with metaphysical topics. This movement will be the foundation for the next civilization, and that is becoming more apparent to people every day. The principles of this movement are spreading across the world and will be accepted by the entire planet.

"The movement has not yet affected the war. This war was put in motion centuries ago and will be played out. The war will end in the year 2027, when the continents shift and much of the current land mass goes underwater. Approximately one billion people will survive to start the next civilization."

"How many?" asked one of the reticent Europeans, in a daze.

"One billion. The planet is going to depopulate."

"You're kidding, right?" Jimmy asked.

I shook my head.

Jimmy believed me. He let out a long breath. I could tell he was affected emotionally.

"What exactly is the New Age movement?" Renan read from his list.

"The understanding of reality—much of what I have tried to explain to you today. We tend to think that nature is separate from us and that it is under the domain of some mystical, separate force that we call Mother Nature. Such is not the case. Our lives and the planet itself are integrated in very complex ways. Not one thought from any form of consciousness goes unnoticed by God. All are interrelated and all have impact, and it is God who is the uniting force that directs everything.

"In simple terms: if the majority of us believe in harmony, then we shall live in harmony. If the majority of us believe in disharmony, then we shall live in disharmony. God simply accepts our wishes. God imagines many scenarios and then directs outcomes based on our choices. We select the civilization we desire, not God. But then, we are God, so it's kind of a chicken-and-egg question. The bottom line is that *we* create reality. We create the experiences we want, based on our collective beliefs.

"An analogy can be made to a musical instrument. The instrument is God; but God does not play the instrument, we do. It is our free choice to select the chords. Of course, because our consciousness is connected to the ALL, God influences what we play.

Chapter 1 - Ireland

I took a drink of water. The ice had melted, but it was still cold. I felt the conversation was winding down.

"I have said very little about how God affects our lives. I mentioned that every thought is received by God and that everything interrelates. Thus, it is our thoughts that intermesh with God. We choose to either live in harmony or live in disharmony by our thoughts. Thus, it is our beliefs—which manifest as thoughts—that create our reality. Our thoughts are our consciousness. And our thoughts are more tangible than we care to believe. Thoughts are energy. Thoughts are real. God uses them, literally, to manifest our lives.

"We can choose to live by our wills—following our egos—or we can live by the will of God. If we choose God, then we can live by trust and love. We can trust that our lives are pre-planned and divinely ordered. This allows us to embrace the outcome and be accepting of what comes our way. This will eliminate or reduce fear from our lives. If we live by love, we can love ourselves and live pure lives, free of temptations. We can also love humanity and the planet, thereby being compassionate and caring."

Renan raised his hand. "I'm not quite clear. God directs our lives according to how we think? We get what we ask for?"

I nodded. "Each of us has a set of beliefs that determine our thoughts. It is these thoughts that create our reality—our individual realities and the planet's reality. *Everything* is determined by our beliefs. God takes the inputs—our beliefs—and determines the outputs according to God's imagination. It's a natural process. There is no judgment involved. Life simply is. It all fits perfectly.

"For instance, we choose to be happy, anxious, or fearful. If we are grateful that God has given us the gift of eternal life and this lifetime as an opportunity to evolve our souls, then we should be happy. We should be happy for every breath we can take, no matter the circumstance. If we are trusting that our lives are pre-planned and divinely ordered, there is nothing to fear. If we live pure lives, only doing those things that are positive and harmonious, then there is no reason to be anxious."

"I think I understand," Renan said. "We each create our own lives, based on what we believe and think."

I nodded. "However, it is not easy to live a pious life. The ego is strong and convinces us that the world is real. It then uses temptation and fear to poison our minds. To make matters worse, most of our beliefs are preset. In fact, we put most of our lives in motion before we are born."

"What do you mean?" Renan asked puzzled.

"We have all pre-selected our lives. We have all chosen unique personalities that are specific to this lifetime. Again, these personalities are illusions, one-time roles. Our personalities consist of a combination of memories of the soul, planetary alignments at birth, conditioning from society, as well as other factors. Our personalities and beliefs are designed for a purpose. We know before we are born what we are going to believe. There is no mystery."

"Interesting," Renan said. "Before we are born, we know who we are going to be, so we have a pretty good idea of what we will believe. And since our beliefs direct our lives, we have a pretty good idea of the outcomes of our lives, as well."

I nodded. "We are all conditioned what to believe by society to a certain extent; for instance, by our parents—but we know this is going to happen before we are born. No one can escape society, no matter where they grow up. However, society serves a purpose. It provides the beliefs that we uniquely need in our soul's development. In fact, we choose a specific life that will instill a set of beliefs that we can use to learn specific lessons.

Our beliefs then provide the experiences that we require to grow spiritually."

"I've never thought of life like that," Renan said, intrigued, finishing the last of his pint.

"Now, what is society?" I asked rhetorically. "It is an expression of God. God and society are interchangeable. Remember, God is *everything*. So, if the society in which we live *is* God, what should that mean to us? The understanding of that truth should change everything. For instance, we should no longer wish to experience war or destroy the planet."

Jimmy smiled. "Lad, if you could convince enough people of these ideas, we could end the war."

I shook my head. "We can prevent the *next* war, but this one is going to run its course."

"What do you mean, lad?" Jimmy asked.

"This is the *last* war. The next civilization is not going to want to fight anymore."

"That sounds good to me," Jimmy said.

"Okay, one last question," Renan said. "What is the New Age movement trying to accomplish?

I contemplated. "Several things. First, it is attempting to awaken people to the oneness of life, which is God. Second, it is attempting to awaken people to their inherent divinity. And third, it is attempting to create a new spirituality."

Renan smiled. "I have a follow-up question. What kind of new spirituality?"

"An individual-based spirituality, with each person determining his or her own unique spirituality, with his or her own beliefs. The only shared beliefs are that God is *all* and that reincarnation is the fundamental reason we are here. Meaning that we are here to learn and evolve. Also, no organized religions are part of this new spirituality; it is strictly individually based."

I paused. "Do you want me to go into more detail for the basis of this new spirituality?"

He nodded. "Please."

"We are God, and God is us. We are part of the God-force, and the God-force controls everything. God is part of you and part of me. In fact, we are one. The perception of separation is an illusion.

"We cannot escape our connection with God. We can attempt to deny our divinity and live by our egos, but God will remind us. That is what reincarnation is about: the constant reminders from God to remember, to awaken to our divinity.

"The majesty of God is that we are all perfect divinity. No one needs redemption, because we are already divine. This present civilization is nothing more than an opportunity to remember. It is nothing more, and nothing less. Once we remember who we are, we no longer need to incarnate."

"Why do we need war to remember who we are?" Jimmy asked, in confusion.

"We have negative experiences so that our souls can experience emotions. These emotions are indelibly stamped on our souls. These emotions we keep; they become our memories. In many respects, our souls are *collections of emotions*. For instance, if you think back on your life, the truly emotional events are what you remember vividly. These were most likely either filled with love (positive experiences) or trauma (negative experiences).

"God is not a being, but *all* consciousness. However, as God's surrogates, we are beings and have unique individualities. God created us to become God's surrogates. We are God's eyes and ears, and our experiences result in emotions and individuality."

"And these emotions cannot be felt on the spiritual plane?" Renan asked.

Chapter 1 - Ireland

I nodded. "Not the negative emotions. That's why the physical plane was created—to feel: fear, pain, excitement, thrill, chaos, panic, turmoil, confusion, madness. And, of course, love. The depth of emotion of love can be overwhelming. In the movie *American Beauty*, there was a line I always remember, "There is so much beauty in the world, sometimes I don't know if I can take it." That was a reference to the depth of love that can be felt—the love of beauty. I know exactly what he was talking about. The beauty of a woman, the beauty of nature, or a child smiling. Sometimes, it can feel so overwhelming.

"Guidance from the spiritual plane is constantly leading us to the experiences we currently need. In other words, we are not alone, finding our way. That's the old spirituality. The new spirituality recognizes that we are not alone.

"Do you understand? God—All That Is—determines our experiences. If you think negatively, then you will get a negative experience. God is always listening to our thoughts—*before ye call, I will answer*—and God already knows in advance what the answer will be."

"What about evil?" Jimmy asked, still confused.

"It appears that evil exists," I said, "but this is only an illusion. God does not consider life evil, because God knows we create experiences for the purpose of soul growth. God knows we are just experiencing and directs the circumstances.

"Are any of you starting to comprehend the complexity? The mass consciousness is the controlling force that interrelates and directs everything. Once we decide, as a civilization, that killing each other is illogical and stupid, we'll quit having wars. Until then, negative experiences will continue.

"Most people are dominated by negative emotions: fear, anger, hatred, resentment, bitterness, dislike. These emotions come from the belief in separation. They do not realize we are all one and all divinity. They deny there is a higher power—God—controlling their lives, and they spend all of their lives denying this power exists.

"It is not wrong to deny God—there is no right or wrong. People simply do not perceive God's influence. Conversely, they are dominated by negative emotions, with fear dominating their lives."

"Wait," Renan said, incredulously. "Are you saying that most people live in fear?"

"Yes. Unless we trust God, we will live in fear. It's possible to simply have faith in God and lose your fear. But it's also possible to know that the world is divinely ordered and that our lives were pre-planned. It will be this second method that sets the world free from fear."

I paused. "A lot is happening spiritually on this planet right now. The war is creating a transformation. What is happening is that the planet's consciousness is becoming more positive, as more and more people become aware. Belief in separation is changing, and the affinity that connects each of us together is intensifying. Civilization is transforming into something harmonious. The Age of Aquarius is almost upon us."

I paused. "I think that's enough for today. Do any of you have any questions?"

They hesitated.

"I have a few questions," Jimmy said."

"Okay," I replied.

"Earlier you said that life is controlled by God. Does this mean that there are laws that God uses?" he asked.

I smiled. "Very insightful. Yes, there is such a thing as God's law. This is also called *natural law*. It is the law that governs the universe. To understand natural law, you must understand that God is All That Is, that God is *everything*. In other words, if you judge me, you are judging yourself. If you hurt me, you are hurting yourself, because I am you, and you are me. All is one, and all are interrelated.

"Natural law requires spiritual awareness, to be understood. But even then, we understand only the basics of natural law. It defines the way we interrelate with each other and with the controlling force that is God."

I laughed. "It's hard to explain in a short period of time. It includes the concepts of karma and forcing your will on another. Basically, God keeps track of our indiscretions and requires atonement. No one gets away with anything."

"Oh, crap," Jimmy muttered.

The Europeans laughed.

Do you have another question?"

"What about Jesus?" Jimmy asked. "How does he relate to everything you've said?"

I smiled. "Jesus was the greatest teacher of natural law who ever walked this planet. Tell me one thing I have said that contradicted him.

"He said that heaven is within our hearts; to never judge another man; to love your fellow man as if he were yourself; to seek first the Kingdom of God; to become pure as a little child; that he and the Father were one; why are you fearful?; of myself I can do nothing. Jesus was talking about natural law.

"Jesus never talked about right and wrong, moral and immoral. He preached love and forgiveness. Instead of this message, the Christian religion was created based on morality. The fictitious devil became the Christian symbol of evil, and all those who reject Christianity are aligned with the devil. People in Christian-dominated nations are either defined as good Christians or bad souls, lost to the devil. This dualism has dominated this planet for centuries, and it is time to end it. Religions are going to go away."

"One final question," I said to Jimmy.

Jimmy looked at me in contemplation. Finally he spoke, "Do people really believe all this in America, then?"

I smiled at his disbelief. "Yes, a great many do. The New Age movement has proliferated in the last decade, as more and more people have become aware. Today, millions of people accept the New Age concepts of oneness and reincarnation. In the early 1990s, only a few million people could relate to the New Age movement. Today, tens of millions believe, and it is spreading rapidly.

"However, not everyone believes this way. You have your war in Europe and we have our spiritual war in America.

"Some Christians think we are pawns of the devil, trying to steal their souls. They are adamant, even militant, in stopping the movement. There is a lot of hatred towards us, but we do not seek to judge them. We understand that they can't grasp the reality of their divinity. They believe in separation.

"It is ironic, in a way. Many of the early Americans were Christians who came to America to escape religious persecution. Now we are being persecuted by Christians for our beliefs. There is even a small militant group that is actively trying to combat the New Agers."

I shook my head in disgust. "Many of my students will not speak in public about their spirituality. They are afraid of persecution. So you have your war and we have ours. These are interesting times, gentlemen."

I rose to my feet. "Well, I guess that's it. It was a pleasure."

I shook their hands, and we all headed out to the bar. They offered to buy me a beer. I accepted the invitation, although I requested water. I had not had alcohol in years.

Chapter 1 - Ireland

We sat at the bar with a few other patrons, and I listened, as they talked about the war in Europe. I was thankful to hear a first hand account, since the AC controlled information ruthlessly.

Most of our reports came from unreliable sources, since it was too dangerous in Europe for journalists. In fact, no journalists were even allowed in Europe. And no news organizations existed in Europe, except those controlled by the AC.

A few freelance journalists remained, but they were covert and carefully hidden. Most had been in Europe before the war began and were now literally trapped. The Internet was still active and they could use it to smuggle out their reports. But they could not get out. And they risked their lives to follow the war. It was a very dangerous profession.

There wasn't much commercial contact between Europe and the rest of the world, either. The war had brought trade to a near standstill. In addition, transportation to and from Europe was very dangerous. It reminded me of the Nazi occupation in Europe during World War II. Thankfully, Ireland was one of the few countries that still had access to the rest of the world.

The AC now controlled most of Europe. Only scattered locations were not under his domain. Ireland and Scotland were among the few countries still out of his hands. The Underground fought the AC's forces constantly. The AC wanted total control, but the Underground was a resourceful, strong, and courageous opponent. Battles constantly raged in Romania, Poland, Bulgaria, Switzerland, Germany, and Russia.

Millions of people had died, and it appeared that millions more would die, as well. The war raged. Nuclear weapons and chemical weapons were in constant use. It was not uncommon for a million people to die in one day. Or for a city to be utterly destroyed. One day it existed, and the next, it was no more. Bloodshed was so pervasive that bodies would literally line the streets. There was so much anguish that people would walk past bodies without even bothering to bury the dead. It was incredible what was happening.

Italy was only a remnant of what it once was. It had been nearly obliterated by nuclear weapons. That was when the war really began, after it broke out in Turkey. That was when the terror started. The AC loved to instill terror. It was his favorite weapon—scaring the world into submission. At the beginning of the war, terror was very effective. America was so frightened that we didn't enter officially for several years. Instead, we stayed on the sidelines and helped the Underground covertly.

Famine and disease were also rampant in Europe. Chemical warfare and radiation from nuclear weapons had taken their toll. Millions of acres of rich farmland, that had once fed the continent, were rendered useless. People were starving. A loaf of bread was very hard to come by. Many commodities were difficult to obtain: sugar, coffee, gasoline, butter. These were either exorbitantly priced or in scarce supply. The living conditions in many parts of Europe had become horrendous.

And then there was France, the AC's base of operations. The AC had recently begun a program which was hatched right out of a nightmare. He'd decided to give everyone an identification number. This number was tattooed with a laser onto the top of the hand. (His number was 666.) Without an identification number, you were subject to death. Moreover, the identification number was required for everything from buying goods to entering buildings.

France was the stronghold location for the AC in Europe. He literally controlled France. The people were under his domain. The Underground did not fight open warfare in France, although it was widely known that they had a formidable presence.

Chapter 1 - Ireland

As I listened to these Underground members, I realized that the American news reports about Europe were fairly accurate, that we were fairly well informed. Asia, the other eternal battlefield, was altogether different. The chaos transpiring in Asia was not being reported with the same determination as in Europe. From what I was hearing, it was basically in the same chaotic state as Europe.

I left the pub and headed back to my hotel. I thought about doing some sightseeing, but then thought better of it. Ireland had been relatively isolated from the war, but I was not comfortable on the streets. I would stay in my hotel room, and then go to the airport in the afternoon. I was here for two days and one night. That was enough for me.

I had lost my urge to travel years ago. Traveling was too dangerous. People were desperate, although I couldn't blame them. It got to the point where I rarely left Los Angeles. At least, at home, I was acclimated to the environment. I could numb my emotions and persuade myself that it was all an illusion, anyway.

Chapter Two

Back to School

As I flew back home across the Atlantic, I tapped on the keyboard of my laptop. I was writing about what I had experienced in Ireland. My visit was blissfully short, and I didn't get exposed to any real anguish or distress, although I'm sure it was there to be discovered.

Most of the people I encountered were somewhat comfortable. I had been greeted with smiles and words of friendship. Underneath the veneer, however, anxiety was unavoidable.

I realized, while tapping on the keys, that my visit was actually not too bad. I had traveled across the Atlantic and escaped relatively unfazed. Such was not the case for many travelers. Many people were overwhelmed by experiences which they were ill-prepared to accept. People would get exposed to pain and suffering, and it would haunt them, or more perversely, change them.

This is why I stayed in Los Angeles. I knew the pain and suffering that existed in L.A. I had grown accustomed to it, from witnessing a steady deluge of human misery. It still affected me, but I had developed a tolerance that allowed me to live a somewhat normal life. I could get up in the morning and go about my daily affairs without letting it affect me. For many, this was impossible. They had become disoriented from exposure to constant chaos, and they were no longer the same.

I know that spiritual awareness allows us to trust that the world is divinely ordered and all is perfection. From this perspective, we can live with joy and contentment, no matter what the situation. I try to follow this credo. But I'm human, and the chaotic world had affected me.

Sometimes, I can rationalize and intellectualize and *know* that my life is perfect, but this can only carry me so far. In the end, it's how I feel. And I *knew* that people were suffering. I *knew*. It didn't matter that I had prepared, that I knew in advance what was going to happen. I *had* prepared, but to no avail.

Except for occasional trips to Santa Fe, New Mexico, I made my home in L.A.; I could deal with L.A. and Santa Fe. In fact, for the most part, I had lived in harmony and joy. I had found a degree of happiness and I wanted to hold onto it. Although, if the truth were told, I was not as content and jovial as I was before the war started.

What led me to this state of affairs in my life? Why didn't I travel anymore? Fear. I could not deny it. But then, we are all controlled by our fears—or else we wouldn't be here on this planet, learning our lessons. If we knew that we were God, we wouldn't be afraid. But then, we would be enlightened, and in no need of incarnating at all.

There are really only two things that dictate our behavior: fear and love. Fear is the antithesis of love, and comes from a lack of spiritual awareness. Fear includes a belief in separation and leads to negative experiences such as war. Love is literally the core of our souls—it is who we are. Love, in a spiritual sense, is more than just feelings of affection, but a connection with the soul. This is unconditional love, and it exists beyond feeling, to an awareness of our divinity and connection to one another.

Fear—a lack of spiritual awareness—was the reason for the AC. The AC was no different from you or me. He was one

Chapter Two - Back to School

with God, just like the rest of us. The AC was the mirror of our fears being played out on a world stage. He accepted that role. Somebody had to fill the part that *we* created. Before the AC was born, he accepted it. Maybe not the pre-ordained role as it had unfolded, but he knew it was possible and he accepted that possibility.

All men who have led campaigns of war and pestilence have played out our inner fears on a world stage. Their roles were required because of our fears. Their roles were destined. Men such as Hitler, Napoleon, and Stalin accepted their roles. Somebody had to do it. We are no different from them. God, in all of God's manifestations, simply *is*. Each soul is equal, as each soul is God. The AC is God, as are you and I.

We manifest our experiences, both on an individual level and on a societal level, according to our desires, fears, and beliefs. Thus, we create our experiences from our beliefs, not God. We create the illusion of evil, not God. And, we have created the incredible havoc that has been released on this planet. We created all of it. When someone pulls out a gun and shoots another human being, they are playing out *our* fears. Evil is the manifestation of our fear. It is as simple as that.

* * * * *

I stepped off the plane and was met by the warm California sunshine. I smiled. It felt good to be home. I thought about the day ahead: I wanted to read today's paper; I had to call Julie at work and tell her I was home; I had to call Jim at our school; and, I wanted to go to the gym and work out.

I collected my suitcase at the baggage claim and headed for the parking shuttle. Walking to the shuttle, I realized that the drive home was likely going to be a headache. The freeways were under constant repair because of the earthquakes. The rebuilding effort was almost nonstop. A section would be rebuilt and then another earthquake would do even more damage.

The shuttle dropped me at my car, and I loaded my bag into the trunk. I headed for the freeway with trepidation and pushed a Van Morrison CD into the CD player. Cars were queued onto the freeway on-ramp, waiting to merge into the slow-moving traffic. This would be a long drive to our condo in Irvine. After listening to a few songs, I pushed eject. Then I called Julie at work on my cell phone, using my handsfree earpiece.

"Hello," she answered.

"I'm home."

"Hi, John," she said affectionately. "I was hoping you would make it back today. Jenny and Ted are coming tomorrow night for dinner. How was Ireland?"

"It was fine. They're in from Albuquerque? Good, I can't wait to see them. How are they?" I asked, in a concerned voice.

"They're fine. I have somebody on the other line ... I'll see you tonight."

"Okay, bye."

* * * * *

I was very lucky to have Julie in my life. I met her in the late 1990s, when I was looking for students for a friend of mine, known only as Teacher. We had been married for seventeen years, and I was still in love with her.

She was strong willed, intelligent, and had an indomitable spirit. She didn't really need me, or any man. Somehow, I'd convinced her that I needed her, and I did. There was too much pain in the world for someone to face alone. You see, not everybody was fine. A great many of my friends had hardships which made me feel uncomfortable. Many people were being dealt a difficult hand.

Chapter Two - Back to School

I was prepared for the crumbling of society — I had prepared. But many of my friends and family had not. Not very many people had envisioned the chaotic world that unfolded. Most people believed that society would amble on and they would retire with their 401K plans and their social security checks. People believed that society would maintain the structure to which they were accustomed. It was not to be.

Most people were caught with belief systems that were no longer sufficient to create harmony and joy in their lives. New beliefs were needed in the face of chaotic change and societal collapse. Many were forced to look at their beliefs for the first time. As society crumbled, people didn't know what to believe. Where I saw perfection and the birth of a new civilization, most just perceived chaos.

From this perception, most people believed in a judgmental God, who was angry. They thought that God's love was capricious and had to be earned by pious behavior. Many felt that they lacked control over their lives, and they were unsure how to earn God's love. Many were totally confused and simply looking for new answers.

Society had not completely crumbled. In many respects, I was surprised by the resiliency of the American people. The economy was in dire straits, but still ambled on. Unemployment had remained over 20%. And many of those who did have jobs worked part time for low wages that barely allowed them to get by.

The society that had survived was a mere fragment of the vibrancy of the past. The war had infected all aspects of life. Hope had faded, only to be replaced by anxiety. Many dreams had been shattered, and almost everyone's life had been affected.

I understood how to let go and let God. I understood that one life — one incarnation — is just a blip of experience, and then we leave the body and go back home to the spiritual plane. I understood that we must love ourselves and accept our lives as already perfect. However, the density of illusion on this planet is so thick that I could not completely see the perfection of life. I knew, but that was not always enough.

Very few could see through the illusion. They were too caught up in it to even consider New Age concepts. Most people still accepted separation from God and from each other as reality. Most believed in evil and judged anything unpleasant as such. I was aware of how others felt, and it affected me. I was aware of the resentment towards me and other New Agers, and it definitely affected how I lived.

There is a saying: if you are aware of a problem, then you are part of the problem. Well, the problem was a lack of spiritual awareness, and it was a big problem. It was *the* problem on the planet. If we could solve this problem, all of the other problems would solve themselves.

The feeling of separation between people and God was rampant. And until this chasm was closed, people would not be aware of their divinity. From this lack of awareness, most people felt alone and vulnerable. The escapes that people had previously used to deny their aloneness—sex, drugs, entertainment, gossip, hobbies—no longer worked. Everyone became exposed. As I said earlier, dreams had been shattered.

Whenever I drove on the freeway, I could feel tension in the air. Worry and despair were pervasive. When was the war going to spread to America? When was the recent outbreak of disease in New York going to spread to California? When was the next earthquake? When was the next round of layoffs? When was the next cutback in vital services or health care? And on and on. People wondered how much longer before life got better. People couldn't get these troubling questions out of their minds.

Chapter Two - Back to School

I wanted to expose people to New Age concepts so that they could relieve their fears and anxieties. This was the reason that Jim and I had started our school. Yet, this was a dangerous profession. New Agers were being persecuted for their beliefs and had to keep low profiles. Having a New Age school was not exactly the way to keep a low profile. However, we didn't advertise for the school, and very few people even knew about it.

My role in this life has been to awaken people to the truth. I had accepted my role, but I was not exactly grinning with joy every day. I felt like part of an underground army, fighting a war against an oppressor, and the oppressor was mainstream society. I felt like a revolutionary in a society that did not want a revolution.

The lack of spiritual awareness had prevented society from reorganizing. It was a catch-22. The answers were in the New Age movement, but the New Age movement was not perceived as a legitimate place to look.

So my quandary was to try and awaken people, although it seemed like few wanted to be awakened. I didn't take this quest too seriously, but tried to help those who were ready and left the others alone. I had faith in God's plan. Like the Bible states: every tear shall be wiped away. I played my little part in the grand plan, knowing that God's plan was in place. Like Jesus said: my burden was easy.

I clipped on my earpiece and called Jim at our school. The school was located in a mini-mall in Laguna Beach. It was situated between a sandwich shop and a drugstore. The large front window was closed off by thick, dark drapes. The front door was always locked, and there was no sign at the front entrance, other than the address number. Entry was from the back door. We always tried to remain as discreet as possible.

The phone rang and rang, but Jim was not there. I tried calling his house next, which was near the ocean, only a few miles from the school.

"Hello."

"Jim, it's John. I just got back in town."

"John! Where are you?"

"I'm on the 405 almost to Torrance. I just got in from Ireland. I should be home in about an hour."

"What did those guys want to know?" he asked apprehensively.

I laughed. "I don't know. It was very strange. I met with four guys from the Underground. They asked me to explain the New Age movement, and our conversation was taped. I think it was for their leader. So be it; it's over. Do we have a class tonight?"

"Yeah, about ten people. Can you make it?"

"Sure, I'll be there," I answered. "See you tonight."

"Okay, bye."

Chapter Three

Know Your Self

Jim and I were good friends. We had taught together at the school for the last three years. He had offered me the position after hearing me give a lecture. It was his school, although he considered us partners. He paid the rent, insurance, and other costs. The revenue did not cover the expenses and my salary. His philanthropy insured that the school could exist.

We taught three night classes per week. Usually we taught together, unless one of us could not attend. We printed a monthly class schedule that was distributed at a few key locations or mailed to customers. Our mailing list included over a thousand names. We charged twenty-five dollars for a two-hour class, which was cheap, but we wanted it to be affordable. Each class was on a selected topic. We taught New Age spirituality, with a focus on spiritual philosophy, which was my strong point. A typical class would include a one-hour lecture, followed by a one-hour group discussion. Sometimes, we would do a group project on the evening's topic.

Classes were scheduled well in advance. For those who did not have a schedule, our web page listed the next class topic and starting time. On most nights, we had ten to fifteen students.

The classroom was somewhat drab. It was a large, single room, twenty feet by forty, with fluorescent lighting and a high ceiling. The walls were bare, except for a big whiteboard in the front and a bulletin board covered with New Age related materials and activities. There were eight tables evenly distributed throughout the room, with four chairs per table. Each table was designated a group during group projects. There was also a big computer screen and laptop computer that were used often.

The atmosphere during classes was relaxed and informal. The only rules were: no smoking, no drinking, and no rude behavior. We worked hard to make the classes as enjoyable as possible, even fun. We wanted people to come in smiling and leave smiling.

* * * * *

I opened the class with a brief introduction and welcome, and explained that printed copies of the night's material were available in back of the room. Then I opened the laptop computer and pulled up my first PowerPoint slide, and began to speak.

Know Yourself

- Astrology
- Numerology
- The Science of the Cards
- The Michael Teachings
- Spiritual and Psychic Readings
- Hypnotic Regressions
- Life's Purpose

"Know yourself. This is where it all begins, in my opinion. Until you know who you are and why you are here, I don't think you can truly find your soul. The reason why is because you need a foundation. You need to know who you are and why you are here before you can communicate clearly with the soul. The soul has a much clearer perspective on why we are here, and we need to match that perspective in order to communicate clearly.

Chapter Three - Know Your Self

"This isn't that difficult, although it will take some time, perhaps years. During this foundation building, we will make contact with the soul. However, until the foundation is solidly built, we will be at a disadvantage. The soul will know our purpose, who we are, and why we are here. But we will still be trying to figure that out. Once we are on the same page with the soul, it will be as if we have found home.

"Before going into detail, let me preface this material by mentioning that these are just tools that you can personally use to help you find your soul. They are not the *only* way to learn about your identity and purpose for this lifetime. Also, these tools can be misinterpreted, and for this reason are often criticized as unreliable.

"Tools like astrology and numerology are not precise, and must be used with a degree of skepticism. Those who employ these esoteric tools do *not* secretly know everything about us. However, these sciences can give us insights. They can help give us clarification about our identity and help us to understand our life's purpose. How? By giving us clues. Who you are right now points to where you're going."

I paused briefly while someone arrived late and found a place to sit.

"Astrology. I think the starting point in understanding ourselves can be found in our natal horoscope, which coincides with the planetary positions at our time of birth. Ideally, you want to have your natal horoscope read by a professional astrologer. When I had mine read back in 1990, it was an eye opener. She told me that no one cared for what I had to say in America, and she wasn't sure why I was here. She said that I should be living in India in a monastery. However, she also said that my horoscope was amazing and incredible and had an almost limitless

37

potential in the realm of spirituality. That was my first clue for understanding my life's purpose.

"From astrology, I learned about my personality traits. For instance, I am Pisces, with Cancer rising, and my moon is in Sagittarius. This makes me a double water sign, which makes me extremely emotionally sensitive. I can feel life and am concerned about the well-being of others and the planet. Being a Pisces, I am a creative person and need to explore my creativity, which I have done through writing. Also, Pisces souls are comfortable with spirituality because they are daydreamers and communicate easily with the subconscious. My Sagittarius moon makes me philosophical, and has influenced my spiritual writing. Knowing all of these things about myself has been very helpful in understanding my spiritual path.

"The depth of knowledge that you can learn from your natal horoscope is stunning and this is something that everyone should do."

I paused and took a drink of water from a bottle that was on a table near where I was standing.

"Numerology is just as powerful as astrology for understanding ourselves. Dan Millman's *The Life You Were Born to Live* is the best numerology book I have read. In his system, I am a 28, which is derived by adding my birthday: 1+9+6+0+3+1+8 = 28. And when you add 2+8, you get my lifepath, which is a 1. Your lifepath is an integral part of who you are and just as impacting as your astrological sun sign. If you don't know what your lifepath is, or what it means, you don't know much about yourself. Being a 1, I take initiative and I am constantly striving to achieve my goals. I've used that 1 energy to write eleven books. I keep going and going, and that is what 1 lifepaths do.

"Another good numerology book is *Glynis Has Your Number*, by Glynis McCants. In her system, you have five numbers. These

Chapter Three - Know Your Self

provide amazing insights into who we are. My numbers are 1,3,5, 8 and 9. This makes me much more compatible with people with odd-numbered lifepaths. And when you read the energy of each of these numbers, you get an understanding of what motivates and drives my behavior. One last comment on Glynis' book; it is amazingly good at finding compatibility between two people."

I paused and scanned the room.

"From using astrology and numerology, I thought I knew myself. Then I met Marilyn, who introduced me to The Science of the Cards, and specifically to two books by Robert Camp. When I found out about this system and how I fit so perfectly as a 5 of Diamonds, it was an awakening experience. It was very detailed, and I felt much more like a 5 of Diamonds than a Pisces. When I read the description of a 5 of Diamonds, I said, 'That's me!' The accuracy of this system is amazing. Everyone should know their card and what it means.

"The Michael Teachings help us to understand reincarnation and where we are on our spiritual journey. For instance, using the Michael Teachings, I found out through a reading that I was a 5th-level old soul, with a role of Priest and Scholar. That was in 1991, and I can't tell you how closely I fit that reading. The Michael Teachings helped me to more clearly understand my life's purpose. There are many other books on this subject and many resources on the Internet. If you want to understand how reincarnation works, this material will explain it.

"Once I put all of these together—astrology, numerology, The Science of the Cards, and The Michael Teachings—I truly knew my ego personality. This was the personality that I had chosen for this lifetime. This knowledge helped me to understand who I was, but not necessarily *why* I was here."

I paused and had another drink of water.

"After you have a good understanding of your ego personality and what drives you, you can attempt to understand your life's purpose. We all have spirit guides who know much more than we do, and spiritual or psychic readings can help us speak with them. I have had several readings, and they have definitely helped me to understand my life's purpose. They helped me to understand why I am on this planet and what I am here to do. Everyone has access to this knowledge, if they are willing to look for it.

"I also recommend hypnotic regressions to experience past lives, and life-between-life (or LBL) regressions to find out your life's purpose. There are hundreds of LBL practitioners across the country whom you can find on the Internet. And nearly every large town has someone who practices hypnotic regression.

"In most cases, we can't truly begin a spiritual path until we know our life's purpose. Until then, our spiritual paths will be unclear. Yes, we can search for spiritual answers and call this a spiritual path, but without knowing thyself, it is a cumbersome path. Once you understand your ego personality and your life's purpose, then you are ready to find your soul and begin a spiritual path."

We ended the class with a lively group discussion and some detailed exercises in astrology and numerology.

All in all, we'd had a very congenial group, and the entire evening went smoothly, as usual. The people who had chosen to come were here because they really wanted to learn, and they were very open to the material that we had to teach them.

* * * * *

When I arrived home, Julie was waiting for me at the door and gave me a big hug and kiss.

"I missed you," she said lovingly.

Chapter Three - Know Your Self

"I know you didn't want me to go, but it was something I felt I should do for Jenny and Ted."

We walked inside and sat down near each other on the sofa.

"Tell me what they wanted to know?" Julie asked.

"They just asked me to explain the New Age movement in America for their leader. They taped the conversation and they are going to give it to him. It lasted about an hour and that was it."

Julie was agitated. "I still want to know why they asked you to go. They know other people who are part of their movement who could answer that question."

"I know why," I said calmly. "The Underground leader asked for me. He is a friend of one of my old students."

Julie was stunned. "Now you're scaring me. Nobody even knows the identity of the Underground leader!"

"It's okay, Julie. It's not like I actually met with their leader. I have no intention of joining the New Age movement or doing anything else for them. This was a one time favor."

"How can we predict what will happen?" she said fearfully. "If this mysterious leader wants to see you, he will find a way."

I smiled. "Is he going to come to America? I don't think so. And I'm not going back. Everything is going to be fine. This ends here. I'm not going to do any more business with the movement."

"I hope you're right, but I am afraid to hear what Jenny and Ted have to say tomorrow."

She gave me a look that said she didn't think this was over yet.

Chapter Four

Jenny and Ted

The next morning, Julie was already gone to work when I awoke. It felt good to be home in our peaceful condo complex. Julie and I had lived there since I began teaching at the school.

She was a graphic artist for a local advertising agency in Santa Ana. She worked eight to five. I would never have imagined our lives being so orderly amidst the chaos that was sweeping the planet, but many Americans like Julie and I had somewhat orderly lives. It was amazing to me. I had anticipated that everyone's life would be severely affected, but such was not the case. Many people led somewhat normal lives, and were not directly impacted in any great way by the events transpiring.

I sat down in my favorite recliner and began reading the newspaper. The big story was the mysterious disease that had recently broken out in New York City. People were dying like flies — hundreds per day. The U.S. government had quarantined the city, and no one was allowed in or out. People were beginning to starve, because not enough food was getting in. It was quickly becoming a catastrophe.

The next article I read was about the continuing food shortages throughout the country. The weather changes had affected the farm belt in the Midwest, and grain shortages were announced. This would cause a rippling effect throughout the food chain. Meat, cereal, milk, eggs, and so on would be affected. It was becoming increasingly common for crops to fail due to the weather. The nuclear weapons exploding in Europe were playing havoc with the weather, as were the continuing issues related to global warming.

America was fortunate, because there was usually enough food to go around. Yes, there were constant shortages and rationing, but, on the whole, you could find food. Such was not the case throughout the world. Crop failures were a common occurrence, and no longer were nations such as America coming to the rescue. America was no longer the great food exporter that it once had been. Ever since the war started, America rarely had a large surplus to export.

None of the other articles caught my attention. I put on my gym clothes and headed out the door. When I returned from the gym, Julie's car was home. I parked with a smile and made my way to the front door. I found her in the kitchen, where she met me with a big kiss.

"Jenny and Ted will be here any minute," she said. "Hurry up and take a shower, and I'll finish making dinner."

"I'll be right down," I replied, as I walked up the stairs to our bedroom.

"I'm worried about what they are going to tell us," she said apprehensively, from the bottom of the staircase.

"Don't worry, Julie. I'm not getting involved any further with the movement."

As I took my shower, I was feeling unsettled for the first time that day. There were some unanswered questions, and I really didn't want to know the answers. For instance, how did the leader of the Underground contact Ted and ask him to send me? And what were Jenny and Ted, two of our closest friends, doing here to greet me? Was it just a coincidence? Or was Julie's intuition right?

Chapter Four - Jenny and Ted

I finished dressing and went downstairs. I heard Jenny and Ted talking with Julie, as I made my entrance with a smile.

"It's good to see you two..." I began, before being interrupted.

"John!" Jenny said, rushing towards me. "How are you? I want to hear about Ireland."

They both approached. Jenny was first with a hug and a kiss on the cheek. Then Ted and I hugged and smiled at each other warmly.

Everyone had the giddy feeling that one feels in the presence of close friends after a long separation. I, however, had pressing ideas that were consuming my attention.

"Everybody, sit down for dinner," Julie said sternly. "It's ready."

We all sat down and began passing plates. I waited for them to explain why they were here, but they wanted to hear about the trip, and so I told them. Then we talked about the disease in New York and other small talk about the economy. I tried to gauge any anxiety that either may have felt, but they were both relaxed. If they had misled me about the trip, they weren't showing any signs of apprehension.

Finally, we finished dinner and made our way into the living room. I would give Ted about five more minutes to explain why they had come, or else I would start asking questions.

Everyone found a comfortable place to sit. I looked at Jenny with an inquiring stare. She noticed my look of inquiry and quickly glanced at Ted. All four of us played this little game of waiting for someone to speak.

"Why did John have to go to Ireland?" Julie asked.

Jenny and Ted looked at each other.

Ted broke the silence. "The trip to Ireland was very significant," he said, in a careful and serious tone. "People were involved who have had little, if any, contact with the New Age movement until now. Those people included members of the U.S. government and the European Underground. For the first time, we are being recognized as a legitimate organization. And, as you know, we have been waiting for a breakthrough like this for years."

"Why didn't you tell me about this before?" I interrupted.

Ted hesitated, and seemed to be hiding something. The tension in the room was overbearing. "You wouldn't have gone, and this was too important," he said. "Our movement has always been identified as either illegitimate or downright occult. We have been defined with many labels, and most of them have been negative. We are perceived by the mainstream as fringe lunatics, with nothing to offer society except bizarre beliefs that have no substance. We are the outsiders who are being persecuted and ignored. We are the present-day pariahs. Now, finally, this is beginning to change. Every day, more and more people hear a friend espouse New Age beliefs. It is only a matter of time now before we finally become a legitimate organization!" He was definitely beginning to sound defensive.

"Why are you telling me something that I already know?" I was calmer, but becoming impatient and annoyed. "Ted, what aren't you telling us?"

"Events were put in motion by your trip. *You* are now a key figure in the movement. The government has decided to release *your* name to the press."

"What?" I exclaimed, incredulous and clearly agitated. So this was the big secret.

Julie was tumultuous, nearly shouting. "How did this happen? Ted! How on earth did this happen!"

"Both of you, please relax," Ted said, regaining his composure. "Everything is going to be fine. Just let me explain what has happened."

Chapter Four - Jenny and Ted

Julie let out a long, frustrated breath and leaned back on the sofa, accepting his peace offering.

"The government came to us last month with a proposition. As you know, we have been waiting for a dialogue for many years. A group of the leaders, myself and Jenny included, sat down with three officials in the administration. They agreed to formally announce the legitimacy of the New Age movement. In return, they wanted us to come clean with the names of prominent members of the movement. They didn't want us to hold back any names. They know that many New Agers want to remain anonymous. But they wanted us to be upfront, and not a secretive organization."

"And they don't have any secrets?" Julie asked contemptuously.

Ted ignored Julie and looked directly at me. "The trip that you made placed you on their list. I'm sorry, but it was unavoidable. We had to send you. The government said that, without you going, it was a deal breaker. I don't know why they wanted you so badly."

All of this was so ludicrous that I laughed and broke the tension in the room. "I do. The Underground leader asked for me. It was his request that I come, and the government desperately wants a dialog with *him*. The government has been trying to build a relationship with the Underground for years. However, the leader of the Underground has little respect for our government, and he doesn't trust them. The government is desperate to find a way to communicate with the Underground. Without a relationship with the Underground, our government can't help fight the war.

"I was their pawn," I continued, "but I don't see what the government accomplished."

There was silence, as everyone thought about what had happened.

"Why would the Underground leader ask for you?" Jenny asked.

"One of my old students is a friend of his," I replied. "They said they call him New Ager. It has to be Raymond Jennings. He always told me that he would fight the antichrist, and he fits the description of being loquacious."

"I'm sorry, John," Ted said, "that I didn't tell you everything I knew before you left. The government told me not to. They didn't think you would go, if you knew the government was involved. I could tell you that I was against this conspiracy to manipulate your life, but that wouldn't be true. I agreed with the other leaders. We decided to ask you to go, and then deal with the ramifications later. You have to understand that we are just as desperate in finding ways to create a dialogue with the government as the government is with the Underground."

I nodded, accepting his explanation, still thinking about all that had occurred.

"So, now that you know everything, how do you feel?" he asked, in a tone that was filled with emotion and trepidation that he had lost a friend.

I hesitated.

"I'm upset," Julie said indignantly. "I can't believe what I'm hearing. I can't believe it! Tell me you're making this up!"

I placed my arm around Julie to get her to relax. "You said that I was now a key member of the leadership. What does that mean, Ted?"

"The government is going to release ten names," he said in a somber tone. "Not only names, but complete dossiers. The press is going to tell the public everything about us. Our education, our work history, what we are doing now, even details on our

Chapter Four - Jenny and Ted

families. Everything goes public. I'm sorry, but that's how it has to be."

Julie was turning red and was absolutely livid. I had never seen her this angry.

Ted continued, avoiding Julie's stare. "After this occurs—probably next month—you will officially be a member of the movement's leadership. It doesn't mean that you have to come to the meetings. You don't even have to call yourself a leader. The bottom line is that everyone is going to perceive you as such. Your words are now going to carry responsibility. People are now going to listen to you attentively.

"As you know, the movement is about knowledge, about releasing knowledge. We want people to begin to understand that separation is an illusion, and it is the leaders that the public will listen to. You are going to be one of the spiritual leaders that people pay attention to.

"Changes are going to begin happening very rapidly once we are legitimized. The leaders are going to start a New Age political party soon, and help New Agers run for office. We are also going to start a national magazine, which is going to support the New Age party. There are a lot of plans in the works. We have been preparing for this breakthrough."

He looked at me inquiringly. "You haven't said much, John. What is your reaction?"

I let out a deep breath. "I hope it turns out the way you expect. Your expectations are very high. To date, the government has denied our legitimacy completely. Not only have they denied our legitimacy, they have said we are a threat—a threat, mind you—to the foundations of democracy. The mainstream population is extremely apprehensive about our beliefs. The fear in society is not timid; it is extreme. And now you say that the government is going to *back* the movement. I find this difficult to believe."

"I know how it sounds," Jenny began, "but it's true. The government is going to recognize our legitimacy. We have read the press release that will go along with the names and dossiers. It reads like an apology. The movement will be revealed in a very positive light.

"I do not know what changed the government's mind," she continued. "I suppose that it's time for us to go public. People are starting to realize that what we are saying is not so far out, after all. My goodness, even the leader of the Underground wants to hear about the movement."

"The government," Ted added, "has a lot of respect for the movement. They told us that we were growing, and that it was only a matter of time before we would begin to change society. They said we were a historical force that was not going to be denied."

I smiled. "I understand what you did. And I'm not angry."

"I am," Julie said, her face still red.

"I'm a bit shocked, but not angry," I said. "If the New Age is going to come out of the closet, then I suppose I'll join you. However, I don't think politics is the answer, and I'm not going to get involved in that. In fact, I would rather avoid any government interaction at all."

"You can stay right here in Irvine, John," Ted said. "We're not going to manipulate you any more."

"You'd better not!" Julie said, in a threatening manner.

"We appreciate what you did," he continued, "and we will always respect you for that."

"We're really sorry, Julie," Jenny said. "This won't happen again."

Julie did not reply.

They did not stay much longer. I think they wanted to leave us alone and let Julie relax. She didn't accept their explanations.

Chapter Four - Jenny and Ted

In fact, she thought there was still more to this than we had been told. She was adamant that it was going to get worse and that we were being manipulated.

After they left, Julie and I talked for more than an hour. I told her that no one could do anything to our lives that we didn't want. If we wanted harmony, then we would have it. If we wanted struggle, then we could have that, too. We choose what we want. It only appears that our lives are manipulated capriciously by forces out of our hands. In fact, our lives are perfectly ordered, according to our needs and beliefs.

After listening to me explain the mysteries of life for awhile, she calmed down. She even laughed. She had heard this all before. But in the last few years, she had not been on a spiritual path. She had not studied New Age ideas for some time. She had become immersed in her job.

I laughed with her and told her that she had put us all through a test of fear. I had passed and I thanked her for the opportunity she had provided. I didn't judge Jenny and Ted, or the other leaders, for what they had done. If they thought it was the right thing to do, then that was fine with me, although I probably wouldn't do them any more favors like this one.

Jenny and Ted were also put to the test. Their test was actually more difficult than my own. No wonder they left so early. Julie had forced them to re-think their decisions. One of the tenets of New Age belief is that you shouldn't force your will upon another. In other words, you should live your life and not someone else's. In theory, they had stepped over the line. They knew it, and I knew it, and Julie knew it all too well. They were supposed to tell me more about the trip before I went, and should have been honest. By forcing their will upon me, they had created negative karma. Julie forced Jenny and Ted to realize that their actions were hypocritical to what they were espousing.

By the time Julie and I had finished our conversation, we were both smiling. We both recognized that negativity is okay. After all, none of us are completely positive, and the planet itself is enraptured with negative energy at this time. In fact, we are currently using negative energy as an opportunity to experience the lessons we have come to learn. There is no reason to get upset when negative energy impacts our lives. That is why we're here.

CHAPTER FIVE

The Announcement

Two weeks later, the announcement was made. After years of ridiculing the New Age movement, the government went public with their new position. At the daily government news briefing, a spokesperson handed out the dossiers of ten New Age leaders, and then proceeded to portray the New Age movement in a favorable light.

The spokesperson called us the "spiritual underground," and said it was time for us to come out of the closet. He acknowledged the growing popularity of the New Age movement and implied that it was too important an organization to remain secluded.

He said the leadership members of the movement were not formally elected, but did exist as a council. This council formally coordinated New Age events across the country, and they were spreading New Age ideas.

Then he shocked reporters in the crowd by saying that we were a welcomed element in society and a positive force for change. Next, he talked about the positive characteristics of the movement.

"The leaders of the movement are not fanatics. They are spiritual people, in a very positive sense. They hold some of the highest values that mankind can hold. Values such as equality, fairness, kindness, and unconditional love. They believe in humanity and the betterment of mankind."

The reporters in the room were stunned. Many scribbled quickly on pads with looks of disbelief.

"Many have labeled New Agers as evil and in partnership with the devil. We don't accept this view. Yes, they believe in reincarnation. Yes, they do not believe in the duality of good and evil. Yes, they believe that all people are eternal. We understand that these beliefs are not currently accepted by most Americans. However, these beliefs should not exclude them from society. These beliefs should not lead to the persecution of New Agers. We think the time has come to cease judgment of New Agers and to end their persecution.

"Last year, more than a hundred New Agers were killed at the hands of Christians. Many believe these deaths were justified in some war against evil. We do not. This government shall not tolerate it anymore. We hereby announce the legitimacy of the New Age movement, and the legitimacy of the New Age Council.

"We announce today that the New Age Council shall be recognized by this government as a legitimate spiritual organization. We intend to seek out their views and include their opinions in public discussions. If we are going to have peace in America, then all spiritual groups must be included in that peace.

"Many of the same people, who claim they want peace in Europe, desire a spiritual war here at home. Many Christians believe that genocide is an acceptable solution. They don't call it genocide, but a religious war. We don't see the difference. What has the New Age movement done to deserve genocide? What kind of values do people hold to make genocide an acceptable solution? These are American values? We strongly disagree."

The reporters looked at each other, unsure if what they were hearing was a ruse. Many were talking with each other with looks of alarm.

Chapter Five - The Announcement

"Many are against the validation of the New Age movement. Many have pre-judged the movement and found it lacking. Well, this administration disagrees. We welcome the positive force that the New Age movement will provide. We welcome their growth, and their influence in society.

"We believe the New Age movement is not a religious organization at all, but a spiritual movement—a way of life—and we accept the values of this movement. This is the one group who *really* wants peace on Earth. After all, they believe in the concept of oneness—that we are all *one* consciousness. And they believe that any perceived division among us is only an illusion. It is time for these laudable ideals to become part of the public discourse."

A reporter stood and shouted. "You can't be serious! These are New Age lunatics!"

The spokesperson held up his hand. "Please save your questions for after the announcement. And, yes, we are quite serious." He paused and then continued reading from his text.

"Until now, the New Age movement has been isolated—in fact, forced underground. Yes, it has been a booming business, and it is prevalent on television and the Internet. But on the political scene, in the public arena, the movement has been non-existent. New Age politicians do not talk about their beliefs in public. People, in general, do not talk about their New Age beliefs in public. Why? Because of fear, and the ongoing persecution. New Agers are targets of attack, and this must cease immediately.

"We have had war in Europe for seven years, and there is no end in sight. You would think the loss of life would bring people together here at home, but such is not the case. There is division and anger in America—group against group, and class against class. And if the war ended tomorrow, the religious war that is raging in America would soon come to the surface.

"The New Age leaders espouse equality, a oneness of all mankind. They say to love each other because we *are* each other. Why does this message have to be persecuted? Wasn't this the same message that Jesus brought? Didn't Jesus say to love your neighbor as if he were yourself? What happened to that message of compassion and humanity?"

Many of the reporters were now in a confused daze. Many were shaking their heads in disgust. One even got up and walked out, mumbling that the president had lost his mind. However, most of the journalists were intrigued by this historic event and meticulously took notes.

"Today, our society is fragmented into separate groups. People identify with their group. What group do you identify with? An ethnic group, a religion, or maybe a social class? As the New Agers proclaim: when you identify with a group, you create conflict and division with other groups. The leaders of the movement want to expose group identification for what it is—the creation of conflict. They teach that the key to humanity is oneness—non-group affiliation. It is a simple message, and yet a message that will not easily be accepted. If we are going to identify with a group, then it should be humanity—all of mankind.

"If this country, if this world, is going to heal itself and find peace, the only answer is *oneness*. If we can't learn to love each other as *one*, we will continue to hate each other as groups. By excluding the New Age movement from the political arena, we are excluding the one movement that is attempting to bring everyone together. The time has come to shine a light on this movement and accept the ideals of peace and humanity that they advocate.

"We see what Christian values of judgment have wrought. Every week, another New Ager is judged and murdered. Every

Chapter Five - The Announcement

week, another person is killed in the name of God. Somehow, this doesn't seem right, when the people being killed are the most highly evolved people on the planet.

"I thought that it was supposed to be *Christians* who loved everybody. In fact, it is the New Agers. It is the New Agers who keep silent when another enlightened one is killed. They don't scream and yell for revenge, because they know that revenge is counterproductive. When are we going to take up their example? When are we going to love people so much that, even if they take the life of our loved one, we forgive them?

"Many say that New Age beliefs are wicked, but we don't see New Agers committing crimes or acts of violence. Many say they cooperate with the Devil, but they don't even believe the Devil exists. New Agers have been labeled in negative terms by millions of Americans. It is time to drop these labels," he concluded, "and accept these people into society. Because if we don't, society will perish."

The bewilderment, tension, and agitation in the press briefing room were astonishing. People could not believe what they were hearing. Many sat with their heads bowed in shock. Many looked dazed and confused, and others simply wore a nervous look of anger.

As soon as it was apparent that the spokesman had finished, nearly all of the journalists rose and raised their hands. The murmurs created a roar.

"What does this mean?" shouted a reporter, before anyone was selected.

"We hope," the spokesman began, "that it means New Age ideals will become mainstream. That people who hold these ideals will begin to proclaim them publicly. And that a greater number of people will begin to accept New Age ideas. In other words, we hope that people will start loving each other and stop hating each other."

The reporters continued to stand. As soon as the spokesman stopped, another reporter yelled a question. "Why do you think the New Age movement is the answer?"

"The only way there is going to be peace is if we love each other. The New Age movement is the only organization that espouses ideals that can achieve this outcome. They claim that spirituality should be individual and not group oriented. Thus, they recommend the end of religion. Isn't religion the cause of current world conflict, and the cause of the cultural wars in America? They appear to be the only group with a clue about how to achieve peace."

Many of the reporters were speechless, staring at the spokesmen with their mouths agape.

"These are esoteric concepts," yelled a reporter. "How can you create public policy on such nonsense?"

"The knowledge of the New Age movement is indeed esoteric, but there is something very deep and true to it. When it rings true in your heart, it rings with a sense of knowing. For instance, New Age ideas stipulate that our beliefs create our reality, that experiences are the result of what we believe. I don't know about you, but that rings true in my heart."

"Are you a New Ager?" someone asked.

The spokesman nodded.

"Is the President?" came the next question.

"No, although he is becoming more open minded in accepting the movement. This press briefing would not have happened without his support. Last question."

"Did these New Age leaders agree to be publicly exposed?" came the quick response. "And, didn't this require a bit of

Chapter Five - The Announcement

courage on their part? I certainly wouldn't want anyone to know that I was a New Age leader."

"No, we did not ask them if they wanted to be exposed. These are individuals who are committed to the New Age movement. They are not all on the New Age Council, but that doesn't affect our opinion of who they are. Indeed, these are the people who are changing America, in subtle, profound ways. These are the New Age leaders, and it is time for them to lead.

"About the second part of your question. Yes, we are exposing them to danger. How can we deny that? But we believe the risk is worth it.

"And all of these people chose high-profile lifestyles. Read their dossiers. These are the people who hold lectures or meet in public with a great many people. They do not lead low-profile lifestyles.

"We believe the time has come for the New Age to move forward into the mainstream. It's time to listen to what these people have to say."

"Thank you." The spokesman left the lectern.

*****

I pressed the off button on the TV remote. I rubbed my eyes and let out a long breath. Wow, I thought, I never expected this. I thought I *had* led a low-profile lifestyle. Indeed I had, until now. Now my life had changed and entered a new phase. Now I was a public figure.

Sitting there contemplating, I realized that I had created this reality. I realized I would have to leave my secure shell and wander out into the world. I would have to expose the knowledge of the New Age to a greater audience. It was something that I had been preparing for.

So this is what Joe was talking about. My guide Joe told me, many years ago, that he was here to protect me. He said that I would be involved in dangerous situations, and he would help me negotiate the terrain. Until now, I had not encountered much danger.

Of course! Now I could see the puzzle coming together: the people with whom I had come into contact over the years, the network of friends I had acquired, the intense learning, and the spiritual focus of my life. Every little detail, every little moment. Everything now made sense.

The phone rang.

"This is John," I answered.

It was my partner, Jim. "Have you been watching TV? Did you just watch the press briefing?"

I was still in a bit of shock and trying my best to relax. Being a Pisces with Cancer rising, I tended to feel things more than most. "Yeah, I watched it. What do you think?"

"I think it's wonderful," he replied. "The movement is finally going to take off. I knew this would happen during my lifetime. I've been waiting for the floodgates to open, and now they have." He was clearly excited.

I didn't reply.

"What is it, John? Aren't you excited?" he asked.

"Yeah, I think it's great. It's just that I'm one of the ten leaders who are being exposed…"

"What!" he interrupted in an agitated voice. "How can that be? All we have is our little school. How can that make you a New Age leader? You're not on the council."

"It was my trip to Europe. The government believes they can use me as a contact with the Underground in Europe. They think it's a possibility that the Underground leader might want more

Chapter Five - The Announcement

contact with me, and that somehow they can use me to get closer to him."

I paused. "Actually, I don't know what they think. This is just speculation. All I know is that the government was involved in my trip to Ireland."

"Tell me more about the trip," he said, wanting to understand how his life had just suddenly changed.

"There is not much to say. I went to Ireland and met with four men in the Underground. They asked me to tell them about the New Age movement in America. They said the Underground leader was interested and had sent them to ask me a few questions. I talked with them for a couple of hours, and that was it. They taped the conversation."

"That's it?" he replied. "That leaves a lot of unanswered questions. Like, how was the government involved? And was the press briefing connected with your trip?"

"I don't have all the answers, and I really don't care. The facts are that these events took place, and now we move on. We can't become paranoid and think that we are being manipulated and watched by the government."

Jim was silent for a moment. "You're not telling me something," he said.

I hesitated. "Well, there is one more thing. I found out that the government went to Jenny and Ted and the New Age Council and asked them to send me to Ireland. It appears that I was requested by the Underground leader. Evidently, one of my former students, Raymond Jennings, made an impression on him. Ray moved to Europe several years ago, and he always wanted to fight the antichrist.

"Something about my trip brought the government and the New Age leadership together. Now I've been affiliated with the leadership. That's all I know."

He let out a deep breath of air. "Wow. What an incredible morning. I haven't had this much excitement since the war began. Okay, we'll just play it by ear. If the classes start filling up, we'll look for a new building. Other than that, we will focus on what we have always done."

I smiled to myself. "Yes, that's exactly what I would like to do."

"I'll see you tonight at class," he replied.

"What's the topic?" I asked.

"We have reincarnation scheduled, but we can change it. I expect the news to break and the class to be full. We'll probably get a lot of first timers."

I hesitated. "No, let's stick to the schedule. I'll do the lecture."

"Okay, see you tonight," he replied.

"Bye," I said, and hung up.

* * * * *

Our newly found publicity had affected a lot more than my little corner of the world. After the impressive press briefing from the government, there was a flurry of debates on television about what it all meant.

Some people were quite angry. They spoke about New Agers trying to take away their religions, their culture, their political affiliations—everything they had worked so hard to achieve. They spoke about evil, the AC conquering the entire world, the troubling war atrocities, and how it was ridiculous to just turn a blind eye to them. In fact, many felt that the New Agers were creating division and endangering national security with all of their foolish talk about love and peace, that it was downright un-American.

I kept watch over the TV coverage to monitor the public backlash against the New Age movement. It was interesting to

Chapter Five - The Announcement

see how fear was prompting many people to publically display their beliefs and religion through picketing and protest marches. Many people carried signs, such as, "Jesus died for YOU!" And one of the women actually dressed herself up as Mother Mary, cradling a doll, to demonstrate her devotion. Not everyone was ready for the New Age movement.

Chapter Six

Reincarnation

The class was full, and it was only 5:30 p.m. Usually, nobody began to arrive until it was close to 6:00 p.m., when class began. We had expected some additional people, but this was a pleasant surprise.

"Should we close the door and put up a sign, saying that the class is full?" Jim asked.

"No, let's get out the folding chairs. I never thought we would use them." I replied with a smile.

"All right, let's fill this place up," he said with a grin, heading for the closet.

By six o'clock, there was not a free space on the floor, except for an aisle down the middle. At least a hundred people were crammed together in the room. The group included a wide mix of cultures. There were whites, blacks, hispanics, asians, and many other ethnic groups represented. It was a noisy, festive atmosphere, with many people talking to one another.

I was standing in the front of the class. There wasn't much room between me and the first row of students.

"Hello, everyone. Welcome to enlightenment school, and thank you for coming. My name is John Randall, and I will be speaking to you for the first hour. The subject tonight is reincarnation. In the second hour, we are going to have a group discussion about the subject. Many of you are going to articulate your beliefs in public for the first time."

The room got quiet. Many were wondering if I was going to force them to speak.

I laughed. "You don't have to speak unless you want to. Anyway, that is for later."

I paused and scanned the room. It was apparent that there were many new faces, but everyone seemed relaxed and comfortable. It was mostly a group of kindred spirits.

"This is an appropriate occasion to talk about reincarnation. Today, after years of silence, the government announced the legitimacy of the New Age movement. And because reincarnation is a core belief of the New Age movement, reincarnation has now been legitimized. The time has finally come for reincarnation to be accepted and impact the way we live our lives."

I paused to let everyone think about that statement and to set the tone for my lecture.

"Before I continue on this subject, I want to state that metaphysical spirituality is not for everyone. I want to make this clear, as it is an important point. Metaphysical spirituality, in fact, is currently accepted only by a small minority of the population. Although this is changing, we do not expect that everyone will change their beliefs, and we respect the right of each person to choose their own beliefs.

"Metaphysical spirituality is not a religion, but a path to becoming aware of reality. Metaphysical spirituality leads to enlightenment, the discovery of the true self. Moreover, it is not the acceptance of other people's beliefs, but an ongoing self-determination of what we each *individually* believe.

"Currently, most people in America are Christians and accept the belief that reincarnation is false. This is okay and not our job to change. My point is that we are not evangelical ministers,

Chapter Six - Reincarnation

here to convert the masses. All people have their own choice of what method of spirituality they choose, be that a religion, metaphysics, or whatever.

"So believe what you want," I joked. "You will, anyway!"

Levity was exactly what was needed, and healing laughter broke out among the crowd.

"Everyone is spiritual and living a spiritual life, even if they're not aware of it," I continued. "How people live *is* their spirituality. Claiming to not have spirituality in one's life does not mean that one is not spiritual. In fact, claiming to be an atheist does not preclude a spiritual lifestyle. How we live and what we believe—and we all have to believe something—is our spirituality.

"Religion and metaphysical spirituality do not have much in common. In fact, religion, in many ways, is the antithesis of metaphysical spirituality. Religions are based on a stagnant set of dogmas, the unquestioning acceptance of a set of beliefs, such as the Ten Commandments or the doctrine of the Bible. Metaphysical spirituality, however, requires a constant analysis and questioning of our individual beliefs, in an attempt to become enlightened. Religion is group based, whereas metaphysical spirituality is individual based.

"The general concept of reincarnation might be accepted and believed by most New Agers. But the actual concept—the intricacies and details—is for each of us to interpret individually. There is no individual or organization that can definitively define the details of reincarnation. There are so many unknowns that we each have to answer it for ourselves. Thus, there is no dogma for reincarnation that has been interpreted for New Agers."

A man raised his hand and I called on him. "Yes?"

"That's not true. What about the Michael Teachings? Aren't those interpretations accepted by New Agers?"

I nodded. "Yes, those teachings are accepted by many. However, that does not make them dogma or the definitive truth. Each person is free to find his or her own interpretation of reincarnation. In metaphysics, we don't point to one source as definitive at the exclusion of others. Everyone is free to select their own source. Again, metaphysical spirituality is individual based, and each individual is free to find his or her own spirituality based on his or her own beliefs."

Many of the students nodded, and I continued.

"For most people, just getting up each day and living life is enough to keep them busy for this lifetime. They could not care less about spirituality, the details of reincarnation, or why we are alive. The vast majority of people are not here to learn about reincarnation or about what I call *finding God*. The majority are not trying to find God. Most people are here to learn personal lessons and to prepare themselves for finding God in future lifetimes.

"Thus, I don't think it's important for all people to learn about metaphysics. Quite the contrary. I expect only a minority of people to search for God. For the majority, all they need to do is live their lives and learn their lessons. We enlightened ones should stay out of their way and lead by example. People should be able to believe what they want, without us telling them what to believe.

"I don't mean to imply that we shouldn't help those who seek answers in their lives—that's why I am here tonight. What I'm saying is that no one *needs* answers. We shouldn't think that we hold the truth for other people. Everyone has their own truth, and their own life to live."

Another student raised their hand, and I called on her. "So, if each person has their own truth, there is no such thing as a singular truth that we can all accept?"

Chapter Six - Reincarnation

I nodded. "That's right. A singular truth, or a complete truth, is too complex to be written in a book. For this reason, we each must have our own truth. In fact, our truth constantly changes. We are each on our own individual path to enlightenment, and along this journey, our truth changes. It is quite dynamic. For example, keep a journal and watch how your beliefs change over time."

Many in the audience nodded in agreement.

"There are certain truths that most New Agers have accepted. For instance, many of us recognize that we are divine and that each of us is part of the whole—God. With this recognition, there is no need to go around saving people, when we already are God. God is perfection, and doesn't need to be saved.

"Conversely, there are many who do not perceive that they are divine. From their truth, they perceive a need to save people. This is their truth, and it is as valid as ours. From their truth, they have experiences and lessons, and they learn. The only difference is that we hold different truths.

"Am I making sense? What I'm trying to say is that I don't care what other people believe, and I don't care what other people do. I'll do my thing, and they will do their thing, and we'll let God sort everything out. Everything is in the hands of God, who is the only force in the universe. And, I might add, these hands are very capable. We can relax. Everything will be fine."

I grinned, and many in the audience were smiling.

"Now, let's talk about us—the group who is attempting to find God. We *are* the New Age movement. This movement can be defined as the quest to find God. We are the searchers, and we use numerous methods for discovery. Methods such as reading, contemplation, meditation, workshops, channeling, astrology, and many others. We use these methods for one reason: we are trying to find God within ourselves.

"Most of those who seek to find God are old souls. They have incarnated hundreds, even thousand of times. They seek enlightenment, which is an awareness of the divinity within and without. They seek to live with an inner awareness that provides bliss and complete contentment.

"Enlightenment is an awareness of the oneness with God, and the closer we come to this awareness, the better we feel. Enlightenment is not a fantasy. It is quite real and achievable. We may not achieve it in this lifetime, but we can come closer. We can find joy and awareness in the search for enlightenment. That is our quest.

"Religions, on the other hand, do not believe that we can know ourselves as one with God. Religions are based on the premise that we are separate from God. This premise leads to the assumptions that we are inferior to God and need to placate God with our behavior and beliefs. This premise has created most of the problems that exist in the world. For instance, there is constant conflict in the world today because each religion has a different interpretation of how God wants us to live."

I paused. "Let me talk about mature souls. At the present time, because of the unique time we are living through, many mature souls are seeking enlightenment. Ordinarily, for instance twenty years ago, this would not have been the case. But because of the unique situation that we find ourselves in, many mature souls are indeed delving into metaphysics.

"Many of you in this room are mature souls. You may ask yourselves: "How come I have not sought enlightenment until now? Why is my life now going in that direction?" The answer is because of the circumstances that we are now living in. We are living in a brief moment in time when enlightenment is open to everyone, or nearly everyone.

Chapter Six - Reincarnation

"I want to make the point that mature souls are a long way from enlightenment. For most of you, you are not ready to know yourselves as God, or recognize God in others. But that does not mean that you cannot seek enlightenment. You can.

"It is a difficult path for a mature soul to seek enlightenment. The reason why is because, for both young souls and mature souls, the world is the basis for their experiences and lessons. This is where their lessons come from. At the same time that they are living this worldly life, they can include spirituality in their lives.

"Only the old soul is ready to detach from the world and become enveloped in a spiritual quest towards enlightenment. In many respects, it's more fun to be a young or mature soul at this time. For you can move back and forth between the spiritual and the earthly. You can work and raise a family and be a member of the city council, and, at the same time, you can delve into metaphysics.

"My point is that enlightenment is only a small aspect of your life when you are a young or a mature soul. We cannot expect these souls to demonstrate spiritual awareness, or an understanding of oneness. Sure, they can become spiritual to a certain extent, but they will not achieve enlightenment in this lifetime.

"Now that we have cleared that up, we can turn to the subject of seeking enlightenment. To seek enlightenment, you must acknowledge that God is *part of you* and that all of life is connected consciously. This is the only way to make any progress toward enlightenment.

"Seeking enlightenment is acknowledging that God is not only a part of you, but a part of everyone and everything. In other words, all is *one*. The distinction between our self and God does not exist. It is an illusion.

"This is a difficult concept to grasp, but it is the crux of metaphysics. Our true identity is God. How do I know this? Because God is All That Is. Nothing is separate from God. All is *one.*"

I paused again and scanned the room. Thankfully, I still had everyone's attention.

"God created all souls, in the beginning, from God. God did this to experience life by using surrogates of Itself. Thus, we are manifestations of God. We are clones, and we all have the same source of consciousness. If we all followed our souls back to the source, we would all end up in the same place. Thus, the family of man is not just a concept, it is a fact.

"This source of life, this source of consciousness, exists as an integrated consciousness. From this source, God interrelates with everything and directs everything in perfect harmony. In fact, this is why the world is divinely ordered. Any perception that this is not true is an illusion.

"Think of spiritual awareness as a continuum. At one end is the enlightened soul who always lives in the present moment and acknowledges God in himself and in everything else. This individual has recognized God. These are the enlightened old souls.

"At the other end of the continuum is the soul who has no knowledge of God. This soul lives entirely out of the past or in the future. It does not yet perceive God within itself. This is the young soul, and it will not recognize a oneness with God until this soul develops through many incarnations.

"The oneness with God does not begin to manifest until the mature stage of the reincarnation cycle. Until then, God is perceived as a separate being. Most young souls cannot fathom a connection with God, because the physical plane is so real

Chapter Six - Reincarnation

to them. All they perceive is separation; separation between themselves and God as well as between themselves and others.

"Why do I bring this up? Because a large segment of Americans are young souls, including most fundamentalist Christians. Because it is impossible for young souls to recognize God, there is no sense in trying to expose them to metaphysical knowledge. It is often a waste of time. Most young souls have no desire to be enlightened.

"For young souls, metaphysics is out of the question. The reason why is because young souls are here to develop their egos. Likewise, mature souls are here to develop their emotions, and old souls to develop their connections with God through unconditional love."

Another student raised their hand.

"Yes?" I asked.

"Why are young souls so devoutly religious, if they don't care about enlightenment?"

I grinned. "For most young souls, accepting religion is easy. They are introduced to God as children and accept God and the Bible with faith. This creates a foundation of spirituality that they can use for their lifetime. It is simple, straightforward, and conducive to their life lessons. Once they have that foundation, they can then go about building their identities.

"Other young souls use religion to reinforce their identities. That is what ego is—identity, the personality self that tries to make us think it is real. They want to be perceived as team players in society, and religion is the ultimate team. Religion helps them to establish an identity in the community. Most young souls are more afraid of their communities than of God. For, the community determines identity, which is their immediate need.

"As with young souls, most mature souls are not working on enlightenment. Instead, they are working on their emotions.

These are the people who have lots of drama in their lives. You may recognize maturity in someone and attempt to expose that person to metaphysics. Don't be surprised if the person doesn't want to hear it. If he or she is working on enlightenment, that person will most likely tell you about it before you ask. After all, that person is here to learn through relationships, and he or she likes to share."

I paused and stretched my neck from side to side.

"Okay, let's talk about old souls, which include most of you in this room. When you reach the old-soul stage, the blur of God's existence begins to fade, and oneness comes into focus. Many of you who are here tonight have recognized the blur and want to bring it into focus. This is what seeking enlightenment is all about. It's about learning how to transcend separation, fathoming the oneness of life, and seeing that the world is divinely ordered. Not just in a conceptual way, but in a tangible way that you can integrate into your life.

"I said earlier that enlightenment is acknowledging God within and without. We acknowledge God by being aware of God's presence in our lives. It is this awareness that makes God tangible. And after we recognize this omnipresent power directing the world, life becomes spiritually satisfying. We learn how to tune in to this source and allow God's infinite power to show us the way.

"This is what reincarnation is all about. All of our lifetimes are directed toward the same underlying goal: remembering that we are interconnected with God. It is a waking-up process. And in the end we remember who we are—God.

"Seeking enlightenment is the first step in remembering. It's the first step to becoming spiritual beings, and walking in step with God. It's this first step where we give up decision making with the ego mind, and instead learn how to think with the *heart*—

Chapter Six - Reincarnation

the intuitive part of us that is directly connected to the soul. Thus, a spiritual being is one who listens to Spirit and not the chattering mind. A spiritual being is someone who has learned how to listen to God."

I looked around at all of the inquiring faces. I had never felt such peace before. I could perceive that something beautiful was happening. It felt like the first day of a new era. I had known this day would come, but I didn't know what it would feel like. It felt as if the energy of the planet had shifted toward the light and away from the darkness.

"Today is a wonderful day, because those who are seeking enlightenment are finally having a positive impact on society. Spiritual awareness is growing and expanding throughout the world and is being sought by many. The transition has finally begun to the Age of Aquarius. Spirituality is being awakened across the world. It's a wonderful time to be alive."

I smiled. "Are there any questions?"

"Yes," came a reply from the front row. "You mentioned young souls, mature souls, and old souls. Could you explain in more detail?"

I hesitated. "How many of you have heard of the Michael Teachings?"

About half the class raised their hands.

"For those of you who have not, I strongly recommend that you buy a book on these teachings. Any New Age bookstore will have several. These teachings have been around since the 1970s, when a group of people began channeling a group of souls called Michael. These channelings continue today.

"In essence, the Michael Teachings are about the reincarnation cycle. As you can imagine, I cannot explain the teachings in a short answer, although learning these teachings is relatively simple.

"The Michael Teachings break down the reincarnation cycle into stages. For instance, most of us are either in the mature-soul stage or old-soul stage. Each stage consists of seven levels. I'm a fifth-level old soul. So I have progressed from the first-level old-soul stage up to the fifth level and have two more to go. Each stage requires approximately thirty-five lifetimes to complete, depending on how fast we learn. After we complete one stage, we move to the next.

"An analogy of progressing through these stages can be made to one lifetime. For instance, in this lifetime we grow from an infant, to a baby, to a young adult, to a mature adult, to old age. These five stages of life each hold certain lessons that we learn. It is the same with reincarnation. Thus, at each stage, we learn specific lessons.

"Not only do people experience a reincarnation cycle, but civilizations do as well. In the beginning of a civilization's existence, the majority of souls are usually at the infant stage. Steadily, as a civilization progresses, souls begin to advance. Once the majority of souls reach the baby-soul stage, the civilization reaches that stage. Note that Japan is currently in the baby-soul stage. This is why they are so child-like and innocent. At each stage of the civilization's maturity, the majority of souls correlate to that stage.

"The United State reached the mature stage in 1989. Thus, the majority of Americans are now in the mature stage. This is why we are going through a lot of trauma and drama, and various groups cannot get along.

"If you understand the characteristics of each stage, then you will understand human behavior more clearly. Let me briefly explain each stage. I pressed a few keys on the laptop and my first PowerPoint side appeared.

The Michael Teachings — Stages

- Infant Soul
- Baby Soul
- Young Soul
- Mature Soul
- Old Soul

"Infant Soul: This stage is concerned with survival. Lives are generally chosen under primitive conditions. Our emotional natures are not yet developed. Thus, we our forced to use our instinctive natures and we end up making a strong bond with nature.

"Baby Soul: This stage is concerned with developing and maintaining civilization. Structure and order are emphasized in these lives. Authority becomes very important. Societies are rigid and have strict hierarchies of authority. It is here that we learn how to follow rules.

"Young Soul: Now that civilization has been created and harnessed, the young-soul stage is concerned with ego. In essence, people become concerned with becoming authorities, and worried about how they are viewed by others. Young souls will fear and reject any ideas that limit their identities. They are concerned with bringing about transformation and they want to make things happen. They are often very narrow minded, and they think they know it all. In essence, they want to play God.

"Mature Soul: Finally, the soul is ready for emotional development. Mature souls are concerned with relationships, especially in groups. Relationships become more important than material/societal success. These souls give themselves emotional turmoil in order to learn about emotions and relationships. Mature souls seek to be understood, and this leads to group consciousness. The result is a planet seeking emotional harmony as a group. Mature souls tend to have troubled lives. This is from their preponderance to grapple with emotions.

"Old Soul: The old soul is no longer concerned with emotional development and instead focuses on spiritual growth. This can manifest in simple lives of just being. Old souls have a more intellectual approach to life. They tend to be internalized and detached from mainstream society. They also tend to create their own system of belief. The last lesson for the old soul is unconditional love, towards themselves and others."

I paused and scanned the audience.

"In many respects, this planet is a unique experiment. The anger and fear that are currently rampant are rare in the cosmos. This is not a readily occurring situation, and we are fortunate to experience this. After all, we get to take it with us—with our memories."

I looked at my watch. "That's all the time I have tonight. Sorry, I couldn't answer more questions." I looked towards Jim. "It's Jim's turn. He's going to lead the group workshop, although I'm not sure how we're going to do it with a hundred people." I laughed, and turned the class over to Jim.

After I had turned the class over to Jim, I noticed one of the students leave. I had been vaguely troubled by his presence during my lecture. He was sitting in the back and looking at everyone. He seemed more intent on analyzing everyone in the room, than in what I had to say. He was white, in his late twenties, clean cut, highly intelligent, and looked like he was in the CIA. I had to wonder why he was in the class.

I quickly let go of these observations as I watched Jim get everyone to form ten groups, with relative ease. (Capricorns have that ability.) He had each group discuss the ramifications of an individual seeking enlightenment. Each group was to create a list of positive and negative ramifications.

Chapter Six - Reincarnation

When they were finished, an appointed spokesman for each group was sent to the front of the class to recite their findings. After the volunteer had spoken, the other groups were allowed to comment. It always turned into a serious debate.

This was the first time we had more than thirty people, and something amazing occurred. Everyone started laughing and having fun. I will remember that night for the rest of my life. If there is such a thing as hope, it was in that room.

CHAPTER SEVEN

Santa Fe

For the next two months, the school dominated my time. Classes continued to be crowded, and the popularity only seemed to increase. We had to make several adjustments to accommodate the additional students. We added another night class on Friday nights and had workshops every other weekend. We were considering hiring another teacher and moving to a larger building.

Then I got a call from Ted in Albuquerque. He asked me to speak at a New Age conference being held in Santa Fe the following month. I tried to explain my busy schedule, but he was quite passionate about it, and I relented.

He said this was the most important conference of the year and that I had to speak. A New Age political party was going to be created. He convinced me that my voice was important at this initial conference. I could warn people of my distrust of politics. That got my attention. I had always been adamant that the answer was not politics, and that politics and spirituality should not mix. Maybe this would be a good forum to express my opinion.

The few weeks leading up to the conference passed quickly. Before I knew it, I found myself packing for the trip. Julie was busy at work and would not be coming. In many respects, I felt uneasy about going. On the one hand, I felt an urge to speak at the conference. On the other, I felt the revulsion of being identified with a political organization. But it was too late, anyway. I had already made my decision to attend, weeks ago.

I took a commercial flight to Albuquerque and rented a car for the drive through the desert to Santa Fe. I had driven this highway many times on my visits to see my friend Teacher. Santa Fe is where Teacher had his school.

Teacher and I had studied together in the early 1990s, before he had started his school. Today, it is one of the best enlightenment schools of its kind. He is known simply as Teacher. He uses that name because it reminds him of his duty. The few students invited to study under him never learn his real name.

I had been coming back to his school to visit and give lectures for the past twenty years. As I drove toward Santa Fe, I knew exactly where I was headed. I would stay at the school and visit with Teacher and his students.

The school was located on the outskirts of town, in a sparsely populated residential area. The school was actually a large adobe residential home that doubled as a school. The students—usually there were five at any one time—all lived there with Teacher.

I parked and walked to the front door. It was hot outside from the blazing sun, and the bright blue sky was stunning. I pressed the doorbell and waited. No one was expecting me, but that was one of the things I loved about this school—I was always welcome.

The front door swung open, and I was met by the calm face of a young man in his twenties. His demeanor was a combination of naïve youth, intelligence, and an aura of love and compassion. He waited for me to speak.

"Hi, I'm John Randall. I'm a friend of Teacher's. Is he here?"

He smiled, and his excitement was apparent. He backed up and swung the door open. "Come in. My name is Steve." He

Chapter Seven - Albuquerque

extended his arm, and we shook hands. He closed the door, and we headed down the hall.

"Teacher has talked about you. He has a picture of you in his office. He said that you might show up. How long are you staying?"

We were walking towards Teacher's office. I smiled at his excitement. "A week. How do you like it here?"

He looked at me with sheer joy. "I wouldn't trade it for anything. It's been everything I expected and more. Teacher's great. He's been exposing us to knowledge that is astounding. I feel really fortunate to be here."

We arrived at the closed door of Teacher's office.

"He's inside," Steve said.

I looked at Steve before knocking. "I'll talk with you later. It was nice meeting you, Steve."

He nodded and continued down the hall.

I knocked.

"Come in," was the reply from within.

I entered with a big smile. The room smelled of incense, and there were two candles burning. Two of the walls were equipped with bookshelves that were completely full, stacked from the floor to the ceiling. In the middle of the hardwood floor was a large Native American carpet. On one wall were a poster of a mandala from India and numerous pictures of past students. The shades were closed over the window, but the room was well lit from two lamps. A large desk with a computer and numerous messy pages was in a corner.

Teacher leapt out of his chair to greet me with a hug. "John! It's good to see you! It's been too long!"

Teacher was half Indian, and his face had sharp, distinct features. He was tall—six feet five—and thin. He had long, straight, black hair that he wore in a ponytail. His presence was striking, with his intensely piercing blue eyes. When he looked at you, he had your attention. He always wore turquoise and silver. Today, he had on a beautiful bracelet, along with a medallion hung from a silver chain.

We met in a warm embrace and hugged each other tightly. I had not been to the school in nearly two years.

"Are you here for the conference?" he asked.

"Yeah. Ted asked me to speak." Ted was a former student and a good friend of Teacher's.

"I suppose we should talk," I said. "A lot has happened in the last three months."

He smiled. "Indeed, have a seat."

I relaxed into the nearest chair. We both knew each other so well that we were completely comfortable in each other's presence. Sometimes I had the feeling that I was talking to my brother, although I don't have one.

"How is Julie?" he asked. She was once a student of his, years ago.

"She's fine. She works too much and tends to ignore her spirituality. Sometimes, I think we're drifting apart. How are your students this year?" I asked, changing the subject.

He nodded. "No problems. They're a very good group. How long are you staying?"

"A week, although I'm attending the New Age Conference for only one day. Would you like to come hear me speak?"

He hesitated. "Okay, but what's this all about?"

It was my turn to hesitate. "Where do I start? Teacher, this is all very confusing. Three months ago, all hell broke loose. I went to Ireland to meet with the Underground, as a favor to Ted, on the assumption that there would be no ramifications. In hindsight, that was extremely naïve. I should have recognized the potential consequences before I even went there.

Chapter Seven - Albuquerque

"I met with four guys in the back of an Irish pub, and they asked me to explain the New Age movement. They wanted to know what it was all about and where it was headed. I talked with them for a couple of hours and then headed home.

"The next thing I know, my name is being broadcast all across the nation as one of the New Age leaders. So anyway, my school takes off. Classes have been full every night. Not only that, but it's a different kind of crowd. New people are exposing themselves to metaphysics. There is a change in the atmosphere. The Aquarian Age is starting."

"I take it," he said, "that you are adamantly against this conference? That the only reason you are here is to tell everyone to go home?"

I laughed. "That's right! You know me too well!"

"Well, I'm going to shock you, but I like what this conference represents. I know how anti-political you are, but sometimes politics is the necessary means for change."

"We don't need a political solution," I said. "We need a spiritual solution."

"Wait," he said holding up his hand. "Maybe there's something positive about the New Age movement becoming involved in politics. Why do you think this conference is happening? Why do you think our schools exist? Aquarius. And what is the Aquarian Age going to be about? Love. We are going to create a new civilization based on *love*. How do we do this? We must transform into a new civilization.

"John, politics has to be included in some manner. Isn't politics inevitable? Institutions must be transformed. Why not help in the transformation? Politics is the only way a transformation can occur. If we are going to transition into Aquarius, then politics must be involved."

He arose, quickly lit some incense on one of the bookshelves, and then sat back down.

"I know this argument," I said, "and yes, I'm shocked that you buy into it. We've always agreed that the answer is not government. I guess my vision of the future civilization is too strong. I envision a tiny, limited government with little impact in our lives, a civilization that is truly free. Remember that governments exist for one purpose only: to control. The current government is huge and controls our lives to an extensive degree. We need the current institutions to dissolve, not transform. I want freedom, not a new system of democracy. I don't want a new system. Systems never create freedom."

He laughed. "You're such an idealist."

I laughed back. "I'm a Pisces, a dreamer." I hesitated. "Please don't tell me you're ready to join the New Age Party?"

He shook his head. "No, this school is all that I am concerned with. I will not be joining any organizations — or political parties."

"That's a relief. For a minute there, I was getting nervous."

"Let's go meet the students," he said. "I have an idea. You can tell them about the coming changes and the beginning of Aquarius."

We arose and walked down the hall. We found three students — all men — in the living room, talking. Teacher introduced us and then went looking for the others. He told us to wait and that we were going to have a discussion.

As usual, the three were men in their twenties. There were always more men than women. Teacher told me that too much feminine energy was disrupting. He had a majority of women once, and they took over the school. Teacher preferred college graduates, just out of college. He once said that the mind must be prepared, before it is ready to learn.

Chapter Seven - Albuquerque

Teacher returned shortly with Steve, whom I had met earlier, and a young lady—a Pisces or Scorpio, I guessed, by her beautiful eyes. We all had a seat, and then Teacher introduced me to everyone. He explained about my trip to Ireland and the conference that was to be held in a few days. After he had their attention, he motioned to me.

"Teacher asked me to talk about the beginning of Aquarius—the next civilization on this planet. I've been talking about Aquarius for more than twenty years now. It feels funny to talk about it, now that it is actually beginning. Today, with a degree of certainty, I can say that the transition out of Pisces is almost complete.

"The Piscean age can be correlated with its symbol: the fish swimming in both directions. This symbolizes duality: right and wrong, good and evil. Duality is the doctrine that there are two opposing forces in the universe. This doctrine has been accepted during the Piscean age, and is the foundation of this era.

"The result of duality is morality; and from morality, we get religion. Religions have interpreted the word of God and turned it into morality. As a result, religions tell us how to live and how to behave. In effect, religions exist with an agenda of controlling our lives. Thus, religions limit our freedom."

"God gives us free will and then religions take it away!" Teacher added.

Several students laughed.

"If that were not bad enough," I said, "religions create conflict, lots of conflict. Most of the wars erupting today are religion based. Religions create dogma with their interpretations of how we should live. From this dogma, each religion is in conflict with the other. The irony is that dogma comes from duality, which doesn't exist."

"Duality doesn't exist?" asked one of the students.

87

I shook my head. "Duality is an illusion. This is something that is becoming apparent to more and more people every day. Once this is recognized by the majority, religions will no longer be needed to interpret morality. Because we are all *one*, and one with God, we are free to determine our own personal morality.

"Once all religions are marginalized, we will have peace on Earth. We will have brotherhood, which is the destiny of the Aquarian Age. The symbol of Aquarius is the Water Bearer. This symbolizes the spreading of wisdom, and that is what is occurring at this time. Aquarius is an air sign, and knowledge will be spread through communications and the Internet. There is going to be a great spreading of knowledge over the next generation. After about 2000 years, the Piscean age is coming to an end, as dualism dissolves.

"During the Piscean age the majority of people were young souls. Thus, we can correlate the volatility of this age with the ego orientation of the young soul. Building empires is what young souls like to do. Then they like to have others admire their work. It is much more complicated than this simple generalization. But, in general terms, young souls are concerned with ego: power, status, and individualism.

"During the Aquarian age, the majority of people will be mature souls. The planet evolved to the mature cycle in 1989, and mature souls became the dominant group. This will lead to a group mentality, as the focus shifts from the ego to the heart. Aquarians believe in the brotherhood of mankind, with an emphasis on *equality* and *fairness*. Although today we don't know our neighbors, Aquarians believe in being everyone's friend. Moreover, mature souls like to be emotionally connected to everyone. This is the opposite of the ego-based and individual-centered mentality that is prevalent today."

I paused. "Are there any questions?"

Chapter Seven - Albuquerque

"Yeah," asked one of the students, "If astrology is closely tied with the evolution of the planet, does it also affect the destiny of my life?"

"Yes," I replied, "everything is affected by the alignment of the planets. Have your natal horoscope done by an astrologer. You will be amazed at how much you learn about yourself.

"Astrology goes so far back in history that we don't even know its origin. It's been used on this planet for thousands of years. Soon it will be considered a science, and astrologers will be licensed.

"Any other questions?"

No one replied, so I continued. "The Aquarian Age will be defined by the revolutionary change of Uranus—the ruling planet of Aquarius, the commitment of a fixed sign, and the communication of an air sign.

"If we look at these three factors, we will get an idea of where we are headed. First, let's examine Uranus. This is the planet of change, often disruptive and revolutionary. It's also the planet that urges people to search for answers. Science and metaphysics are the results of influences from Uranus. Revolutionary change and metaphysical awareness are Uranian in nature.

"The Aquarian is the inventor, the awakener, and the searcher of truth. Scientists and metaphysicians are natural rebels. They don't care what people think about their ideas. Their job is to search and reveal. The unconventional is their norm. Going against convention, in the pursuit of ideas and truth, is their modus operandi. And when they discover answers, they release them, whether they are radical, revolutionary ideas or universal laws of nature.

"The key to the Aquarian Age is revolutionary change. This will occur in science, technology, culture, and spirituality. We have experienced the beginning of the technological revolution in the 20th century, but this is nothing, compared to what will occur in the 21st and 22nd centuries. In tandem with that will come a spiritual revolution. New ideas about spirituality are being revealed today, and these ideas are beginning to take hold in order to form a new civilization.

"The foundation of any society or civilization is belief. The currently held beliefs will begin to break down and transform into new beliefs. And Aquarius will bring revolutionary change out of these new beliefs.

"The Aquarian is the rebel, the awakener. Aquarians have strong urges to break from the past. Their independent natures produce urges towards freedom. This results in an insatiable search for answers. This search inevitably leads to the unconventional. They search in all areas for answers. But their favorite is the very old or the very new, the ancient or the esoteric. Thus, the Aquarian is a rebellious revolutionary. He or she is the inventor and the propagator of change.

"The Aquarian age will be a sharp break from the past, and a new revolutionary attitude will manifest. We are quickly approaching this *new* spiritual age. It will be a time when people will learn to live harmoniously together: a true time of wonderment, compared with how we live today...."

"Indeed," Teacher interrupted, "it's already happening. Everywhere, there are miracles occurring on a daily basis. The new children, the Indigos and Crystals, have brought with them new DNA and new inherent abilities. They are already tapping into the 4th and 5th dimensional energies."

I nodded. "That's true. And these advanced souls are impacting humanity and injecting higher vibrations which are uplifting the entire energy vibration of the planet."

"Aren't we also advanced souls?" One of the students asked

Chapter Seven - Albuquerque

"Of course," I said. "What I was implying is that advanced souls are becoming more and more common on the planet. It won't take much longer for all of these souls to impact humanity in a positive way. Once a critical mass of spiritual awareness is reached, everything will change."

"That's why this school exits," Teacher added. "I'm teaching advanced souls to raise the vibration of the planet."

The students all smiled.

"Okay," I said, "the only thing left to explain is that Aquarius is a fixed sign and an air sign. From a spiritual standpoint, the air sign of Aquarius will manifest through communication of revolutionary ideas. This will be done primarily through personal contacts and word of mouth. People will begin talking to each other about spirituality and metaphysics. This is going to be a word-of-mouth revolution, although the mass media and the Internet will be contributors. The airy quality of Aquarius is ideal for spreading these new spiritual ideas, and these changes will occur within our lifetimes.

"The fixed characteristic of Aquarius is that of willfulness and stubbornness. Aquarians will not take no for an answer for their revolution, and once the concepts of the revolution are accepted, the Aquarian will not let go of these concepts. A correlation can be made to the passion of a scientist. Once the scientist gets an idea in his head, it sticks like glue until it manifests. He or she will search and search until that idea comes to fruition.

"Well, that's about it. The only thing that I might want to add is the correlation of a great genius who is going to appear around 2050. He is going to be the greatest scientist and inventor ever. His inventions will transform the world. What is unique about this great genius, however, is that he will explain to the world how science and spirituality are one and the same. His impact will be as great in the social arena as it is in the sciences. This scientist is going to show us that we're God. It should be an amazing time during his lifetime. Teacher and I won't be here, but most of you will experience this."

I smiled and so did everyone else.

Chapter Eight

New Age Convention

The conference was bustling with people. Driving past the front entrance with Teacher, we both realized that this was a major event. There were literally hundreds of reporters and camera crews staked out. In addition, there was a horde of people loitering outside, trying to get in.

We parked two blocks away and walked to the entrance. As we got closer, I noticed the Christian protesters. They were carrying signs and marching back and forth in front of the entrance. We ignored their comments as we walked past, on our way to a registration tent. We quickly received badges and were on our way inside.

It was late in the afternoon, and the conference had been going on all day. The auditorium was crowded, and someone was on stage, speaking from a lectern. We found our seats and sat and listened. I was scheduled to talk in two hours.

Convention fever was high, and the next speaker was a woman from New York. She sounded like a politician, giving promises and speaking in generalities. She explained how a New Age party could make a difference, and that the time was right for a new beginning. Personally, I felt a revulsion listening to her. It was the same old spiel: let's make government work using *our* ideas. Teacher was right—I had come to tell everyone to go home.

The time passed quickly, and then it was my turn. I didn't bring any notes, although I had prepared extensively. I already knew what I was going to say. What I didn't prepare for, however, were the television cameras.

When I agreed to speak, I didn't know the convention was going to be televised. I had little trepidation speaking before the conference, but I was apprehensive about speaking to a large television audience. I simply did not want to be a celebrity.

As I approached the lectern, I felt an intense nervousness, and my heart was racing. "Hello, I'm John Randall. I'm a New Age author and teacher. I was invited today to speak."

I was stuttering from my nervousness and paused to relax. There was a polite applause and someone yelled, "Thanks for coming, John."

I smiled and continued. "Many of you who are here today will not want to hear what I came to say. In fact, right now I feel out of place."

Finally, my heartbeat slowed, and I relaxed. "I'm here only because certain people convinced me that I needed to speak. You could say that I acquiesced. After today, however, you won't find me at any more political conventions. This will be the last time I'm affiliated with the New Age party or with any other political organization."

A few people booed loudly and made disparaging comments.

"All of you are here today to start a new political party—the New Age party. As you can surmise, I'm against it. I came here today to explain why this is not a good idea."

Several more people booed and made catcalls. I paused and scanned the room. More people seemed interested than not, so I continued.

"The New Age movement is about the dissemination of spiritual knowledge. This knowledge will lead to spiritual

Chapter Eight - New Age Convention

awareness and the uplifting of humanity. In fact, this knowledge will create a new civilization. As the saying goes, 'The pen is mightier than the sword.' The government knows the danger of this knowledge and that the only way to control it is to politicize it."

I paused to emphasize the last sentence.

"The role of government is the distribution of power. Conversely, the role of the New Age movement is the dissemination of knowledge. These two roles are in conflict. For, how can you disseminate knowledge and distribute power at the same time? It's impossible, in my opinion. Ultimately, those who distribute power will attempt to control the content of that knowledge. This is inevitable, and Washington knows this."

The boos had stopped, and the audience was now listening intently.

"Politicians decide how knowledge is distributed, based on the desires of their constituency. Those with the most power always influence how knowledge is distributed and how it is spun. Currently, politicians have little power to influence our movement, but that will change if you politicize it.

"My point is that those in power have a vested interest in the status quo, and we are a very real threat to the status quo. The current political system represents their interests, not ours. Do you really believe they want to help us? We are proposing a revolutionary new way of perceiving life. We are revolutionaries. We don't want incremental change. We want a complete transformation...."

A few people clapped, but many were silent.

"In many respects, what I'm saying right now is pointless. For, very few of you agree with me. I can tell you why government is not the answer, but it's not what you want to hear. It's too late to explain, because you have already made up your minds. Even

95

many of my closest friends believe that this new party is a good idea. And, as the saying goes, belief creates reality.

"When I was first exposed to the New Age movement, I didn't think this could happen: that the end result of the movement would be a foray into the political arena; that we would do the same thing that we came to loathe, or wind up dictating new ways to live.

"Any system, by its very definition, will always limit freedom. Politics is a system. As Krishnamurti so beautifully taught us, joining any system only creates conflict with those outside the system.

"I've said it a hundred times: man cannot govern man. It is that simple. Man can only govern himself. He must be left to his own urges and desires. That is freedom. Politics is about the control of those urges. Politics is about the control of free thought and the control of free expression. Politics is the dissemination of power within a system. This is why there are politics in every organization.

"From my viewpoint, it is counter-productive to deny freedom. Anytime you have one human dictating to another human, that is exactly what happens. Our political system is set up to control people, to direct them to live in certain ways. Why would any of you want to join such a system, when we know it is counter-productive to real freedom?"

I paused and took a drink from a water bottle that was on the lectern.

"Let's get down to the nitty-gritty. We are co-creators with the God force. We can use our beliefs to become political or to become truly free. A new humanity is about to be born, and it will not be based on power and politics, but love. For most of us, politics will not be a part of our lives. We will be free to live

Chapter Eight - New Age Convention

each day as we choose, and not within a system that dictates or influences our behavior.

"We need a higher goal for humanity. We don't need incremental change through politics, but revolutionary change. We are divinity. Now that we know this, we can create a new world. All we need are our thoughts, not some political system.

"Thought is connected to the God force. In fact, thought is how co-creation transpires. What we think is what we get, but there is a catch: the God force seeks harmony. Thus, we have the free will to create a political party, but if it is not in harmony, it will not last. And, in my opinion, this party will dissolve. Why? Because man cannot govern man.

"Our current political system is in chaos. That much is evident. How many times has martial law been declared in the last few years? Our government is huge and out of control. It impacts almost every aspect of our lives. It has become a controlling body in the extreme. For there to be peace on Earth, politics must be reduced drastically, starting with the elimination of all political parties and the national government."

I paused again, and a few people actually applauded.

"I can understand your motives, as it is natural to want to influence society in a positive manner. As society decays, it is natural to want to help. But politics is not the solution. To think you are capable of transforming government by joining government is an illusion. In the end, this government will still collapse upon itself.

"There is an answer, although most of you don't want to hear it. The answer is to be a committee of one. Don't join anything. Be your own authority. Learn to make your own decisions. Live outside the system as much as possible. Try not to give the system legitimacy.

"I'm a revolutionary. I'll admit it. I contend that when people vote, they condone their leaders—and their system. What would happen if 70 or 80% of the population quit voting? I submit, the system would dissolve. But this is off the topic, and I don't want to talk about political solutions. I came here to tell you that there *are* no viable political solutions. It's time to wash your hands of politics completely.

"Set an example and wait. That's my recommendation. Wait for this civilization to continue on its natural course of dissolution. This government structure will not last much longer. Why do you think they want our help? It's not up to us to save it. So I say: let it fall."

Although some people applauded this idea, the vast majority were ignoring my plea.

"The current social system is outdated. Why? Because it is based on false beliefs. Today, we are approaching a new era, based on new beliefs and new values—the Age of Aquarius. The new world is going to be a completely new place. It's not something that can be evolved from present day society.

"The freedom that we enjoy today is an illusion. We are not free in a social sense. We can't get up in the morning and do what we want. Why? Because everything is based on economics. We have to get up in the morning and work. Our lives are dictated by money, down to the point of what we can do and say. Our economic culture harnesses our freedom and controls our behavior. How many of us have to worry about a place to sleep and food to eat? This shouldn't be so.

"Look around you. Everyone is judged according to their economic value. Who you are is directly correlated to what you can provide society. Without this value, a person is judged a loser, or a person who needs to get his life in order.

Chapter Eight - New Age Convention

"People are so consumed with their economic identity that they close off their spiritual identities. They live on the surface of life, refusing to look underneath, where reality is shaping their lives. The spiritual dimension of life is overlooked and undervalued.

"Religion is not overlooked, but then religion is not spirituality. Religion is the belief in someone's interpretation of spirituality. In other words, religion is based on dogma. Spirituality, on the other hand, is based on knowledge. Spirituality is knowledge that we are inseparable from God, and all that that implies. Spirituality is Gnostic—a direct relationship with God. Spirituality and religion are not the same. Today's culture is religious, yet rarely Gnostic.

"My point is that you can't create a spiritually based political party in an economic-based society. It's not going to happen. Many of you think all that's required to change society is the communication of our metaphysical ideas, and that government is the best means for that communication. Again, this is an illusion. Until we break the bonds of an economic-based society, there shall be no change. And breaking the bonds is a revolutionary idea, not a political program."

I paused and took another drink of water.

"Change will come from the recognition that we are all one. When you acknowledge God in me and I acknowledge God in you, then we will have change, and not until. Today, our culture is based on denial of spirituality, and that denial shall continue until the government collapses. Once the national government goes, with it will go the ingrained beliefs in separation. A vacuum will appear, and it will be filled with a new belief in oneness.

"As a society, we currently deny our inherent divinity. There are those who are enlightened, but our numbers are small. To think we are capable of enlightening a society using politics is naïve. In fact, the New Age movement is not about evangelical methods of awakening others. We need only to set an example. It's not for us to transform society. That shall happen in due course.

"Maybe *denial* is the wrong word. The correct word is probably *forgetfulness*. We have forgotten who we really are—God. Life is a process of remembering who we are. Each lifetime, we remember a little bit more. Steadily, we become enlightened. Jesus was a great example of this. He said that everyone could do the things that he did. But he didn't say we would do them in this lifetime.

"Today, everyone is hiding their lives from each other because they are afraid. They don't know who they are—divinity. Thus, there is very little honesty and communication in this culture. Everyone is being secretive. Why? Doesn't this question intrigue anyone? Doesn't anyone wonder why fear is so rampant? And that love and trust are so rare?

"Today, people are perceived as good or bad, based on how they contribute to society. But on what terms do we define contribution? How do we decide who is good? I submit that we currently use economic value. For, if society were based on oneness, we would perceive the contribution of everyone. Then we would allow people to be. Our divinity doesn't need to be proven. It is. And politics has nothing to do with this.

"Is it that difficult to comprehend that this civilization is based on economic value? And is it that difficult to comprehend that this is a false belief? To me, it's crystal clear. The end result is a civilization whose days are numbered. It's not a civilization that can be saved. We *have* to start over.

"My point is that we are going to create a spiritual civilization. And it would serve our interests to acknowledge this sooner, rather than later. This civilization is going to be completely new—not a semblance of the past. To acknowledge the inevitability of

Chapter Eight - New Age Convention

the demise of society will create harmony in our lives at a faster rate. To acknowledge the demise will spur it on. All we have to do is wait, and it will happen naturally. Conversely, the more we fight the demise, the more anxiety and turbulence we will feel as the demise lingers."

I paused and scanned the audience. I tried to sense the degree of interest and how the speech was going. The impression I got was one of conflict. Most of the people wanted their new party and had had enough of my speech.

"The next civilization is going to be based on spiritual values. Most of you already know this. So, why the big push into politics? Why am I the lone voice today telling you that this is the negative path? And why the resistance from most of you?

"Our current social system is not spiritual at all. It is based on economic values. Can't you see that the political system reinforces the social system? It's the function of a political system to maintain the social system. Don't take my word for it, check history.

"The Sumerian, Mayan, and Atlantean civilizations all disappeared because they could not change. Their political systems would not allow change. Why? Because that's not how it works. A civilization's social system cannot evolve forever. Eventually, it will cease to exist. Civilizations end and then are reborn as something different. That is where we are headed. There will be a demise and then a rebirth. Thank you."

I turned and walked off the stage. The crowd politely applauded, but the applause only lasted a few seconds. They didn't want to hear my message. They had come to start a political party, not to hear someone tell them to go home and be a committee of one.

Teacher and I left. We didn't want to hear any more speeches about the generalities of politics.

Chapter Nine

Dan

Driving back to the school, Teacher asked if we could visit a friend. He said he didn't get out much, and that this was a good time to stop by.

We drove to a residential area on the outskirts of the city. The adobe homes that lined the streets had gravel front yards and disheveled landscaping. It was a lower-income neighborhood, and most of the cars parked in front of the homes were older models.

We parked in front of a small adobe home and made our way to the front door. The bright blue sky was exhilarating. I looked off into the distance and scanned the desert. It was beautiful here. Breathing the clean air was a welcome change from Los Angeles.

Before we reached the front door, it opened, and a Native American appeared. He wore Levi jeans, leather boots, and a button-down shirt. He had intense dark eyes and reminded me a lot of Teacher. His hair was also long and black, although braided into a ponytail. I would estimate his age to be at least sixty. He smiled at Teacher and opened the door to let us in. I could tell from the informality that they were close friends.

I found it interesting that Teacher had never mentioned him before. I wondered if they were relatives. It seemed likely.

As we entered the house, Teacher and his friend hugged and smiled at each other. Then I was introduced. His name was Dan.

We shook hands, and then the three of us walked into the living room. He sat down in a chair, while Teacher and I shared the couch.

It was a three-room house: living room, kitchen, and bedroom. He lived simply. The furniture was old and basic. There was very little decoration on the walls. I spotted one small picture of a desert nature scene. The dust on the twenty-inch television implied that it was rarely used.

"Dan used to be my stepbrother," Teacher said, "or more precisely, this was the body my stepbrother inhabited."

I looked at Dan in confusion. Apparently, Teacher was implying that Dan was a walk-in of some kind.

Dan smiled. "He hasn't told you, has he?" he asked.

I shook my head. "No."

Dan nodded for Teacher to continue.

Teacher paused. "I didn't want to tell you before we arrived. It's better to tell you now that you have met him. He's a walk-in from the Pleiades. He assumed my brother's body about six months ago, when my stepbrother had a heart attack. My brother left his body, and Dan moved in.

"My brother lived in Phoenix, and I hadn't talked with him in years. I didn't even know that he'd had a heart attack. We weren't very close. Anyway, Dan came to visit me at the school three months ago. We've been in contact ever since."

I looked at Dan with new respect. I was excited, to say the least. I had heard of walk-ins living among the population, but I had never met one. I knew that many advanced souls had come to this planet to help with the transition. I had an idea that Dan was one of these.

He smiled at me. "Like Teacher, you have remembered well. You both came with the same goal: to remember who you are

Chapter Nine - Dan

and to spread that knowledge. You have both succeeded. In fact, there is little that I need to teach you.

"I have come to work with both of you. I have come to spread light, just as both of you are spreading light. You have your schools, and I shall begin my own. The three of us will work together. You will continue to send students to Teacher, and Teacher will begin sending students to me—the gifted ones, the Indigos and Crystals.

"Before I assumed this body, I looked down on this planet and scanned for opportunities to help with the transition. I saw what you and Teacher were doing and decided to join you. I communicated with your guides and higher selves, and everything was arranged. You could say that this project is being manipulated by higher sources. But then, isn't everything?

"As I have told Teacher, I know a lot about both of you. Not just this life, but many previous lives, as well. We have not met before, but that is not important. We shall be friends."

I looked at Teacher. What had Dan told him to convince him he was not his stepbrother? "Do you have any reservations about who he says he is?"

Teacher laughed. "Ask him some questions. My brother was not a spiritual person. Dan knows more than we do. He's the teacher now—our teacher."

I nodded with wonderment. It was evident that Teacher was convinced. I looked at Dan. "If Teacher is convinced that you are a walk-in from Pleiades, that's enough for me. I have learned to trust his judgment. And now that I know who you are, I see you as someone I can learn from. It's difficult for Teacher and me to find people to talk with who understand reality. I'm honored to meet you."

Dan smiled. "I am glad that you receive me as warmly as Teacher has. And yes, I came to be a teacher, as well as a friend."

Suddenly, I realized that he was indeed an advanced soul. "You know more than we do? Oh, this is great!"

I looked at Teacher, and he smiled, acknowledging our good fortune. It was an exhilarating moment. We had found someone who could answer *our* questions.

"Wow, and you're going to be our friend and teacher? This is too good to be true. I was told that my learning would continue, but I didn't expect anything like this."

I paused in contemplation. "Can we go out and have something to eat? I already have several questions, and I'm starving."

Dan laughed at my excitement. "Sure, what are you hungry for?"

"Mexican food sounds good," Teacher interjected, knowing that is what we each liked.

We all rose and headed for the door.

* * * * *

We drove a few blocks to a Mexican restaurant. We were seated, and each of us ordered from a menu. After our food was brought to us and I had eaten a few bites, Dan asked me if I had any reservations about believing that he was from Pleiades.

"No, I don't have any problem with that. I have read about walk-ins. I know there are people here such as yourself, who were not born on this planet. Although, I thought walk-ins came from the spiritual plane, not from other planets."

He nodded. "Normally that is so. It is unusual for incarnate souls to switch bodies from one planet to another. If it was not for the changes occurring on this planet, it would not have been allowed."

"Can you talk about Pleiades?" I asked.

He nodded.

Chapter Nine - Dan

"Tell me what your life was like, and why you gave it up to come here," I said.

He hesitated. "Hmm. This is not easy to explain with words. I will try, but you must use your imagination. First of all, the civilization on Pleiades is much more advanced and has existed for thousands of years. We exist much like you do, in that we have commerce, an economy, friends and families. The differences are mainly in technology and our spirituality, which has created a completely different culture.

"In technology, we have harnessed the life force for energy. The life force is an inexhaustible energy source that permeates the universe. It is everywhere. It is in the air that we breathe. If you can imagine what life would be like here with this natural energy source, then perhaps you can get a glimpse of our civilization. Pollution, for example, does not exist.

"You must also understand that everyone on Pleiades is spiritually advanced. Everyone knows that the life force *is* God, and that God is the only force in the universe. Pleiadians *know* that each person makes up the whole and that no one is less significant than another. Most importantly, each Pleiadian understands that he or she is part of God. This allows everyone to live together in harmony.

"Perhaps I should say a few more words about the life force. What many here on Earth refer to as God, is not a being. God is a consciousness that interrelates and integrates everything together. Nothing is separate from the life force. All consciousness interrelates and affects other consciousness. In other words, our thoughts and actions impact the whole. And believe it or not, *everything* has consciousness and is *alive*. Not just humans and animals, but air, rocks, dirt, metal, glass, wood, plastic ... everything. That fork in your hand is as alive as we are—it's energy, too.

"Each consciousness interrelates in a kind of cosmic play. Moreover, the physical plane—where we incarnate—is connected to the spiritual plane—where we do not. Whereas the physical plane may create disharmony, the spiritual plane eventually reigns in the reckless adventures of rebellious souls...."

I interrupted. "I thought you were going to tell us about why you came here."

He smiled. "I am. I am getting there."

"I'm sorry," I said. "Continue."

"The life force of the physical plane is interrelated with input from the spiritual plane. All of us have guides and higher selves on the spiritual plane who are giving us direction. There is incredible interplay going on. What we perceive is only one side of the coin. The other is hidden from view.

"Currently, the spiritual plane is working diligently to influence the outcome of this current civilization. In many respects, there is a grand plan at work, and walk-ins are part of this grand plan. I volunteered to help and was accepted.

"Before I go further, I wanted to give you an overall view of why I am here. That is why I talked about the life force and the interplay of the physical and spiritual planes. Now I can talk more about Pleiades.

"On Pleiades, everyone vibrates at a much higher vibration than here on Earth. This high level of vibration is from advanced spirituality. People there are aware of who they are. They also know about their previous lives and the lessons they are learning.

"Pleiadians are aware of the purpose of life, which is the evolution of the soul. From this awareness, they understand how to live in harmony, and respect the gift of eternal life. To repeat, Pleiadians know who they are. No one goes around feeling sorry for being an eternal soul. In general, Pleiadians are content.

Chapter Nine - Dan

"The high degree of vibration of Pleiadians also creates health and harmony unknown on this planet. There is very little illness, and thus there are few healers, or what you would call doctors here on Earth. Our lives are ten times as long as yours. But mental and physical health are not a concern.

"Another important factor is that everyone is telepathic — we can read each other's minds. That is how we communicate, and no one can hide their thoughts. For advanced civilizations, this is the preferred method of communication. It provides instant feedback, which allows insight for spiritual growth. Here on Earth, people are still trying to learn about themselves and what they truly believe. Thus, they hide from each other. Telepathy would be counter-productive here, although it is beginning to appear in the Indigo and Crystal children."

Dan smiled. "Someone should make a movie where telepathy is possible for your culture. It would reveal to people how they constantly judge each other. It would be quite illuminating for people to be able to read each other's minds. People could see how they really think about one another. Here on Earth, many people dislike each other. That is ironic, since they are actually eternal souls who truly love each other.

"On Pleiades, people are much more free and happy. People do what they want, without the burden of having to financially support themselves. Everything is shared, including food and shelter.

"There are social levels, but it is acknowledged that the higher social levels are attained through diligence and are earned. And anyone, moreover, can attain these levels through effort. Everyone selects the social level that they want to learn from.

"There is no jealousy between the social levels. People accept what they do, knowing it is what they need to do. People acknowledge that they are responsible for themselves. There is much more awareness of the *why* of life. People understand *why* they are there. If any confusion or doubts arise, they can astral travel to meet with their guides for assistance. People on Pleiades do not have the trapped feeling that exists among many here on Earth.

"Government is much simpler than it is here. Maybe 1% of the population has a government job. There is so much trust and cooperation that there is little need for government. The government is mainly concerned with inter-galactic trade and commerce. I might add that there is very little crime, and no jails whatsoever.

"The Pleiadians have the option of leaving Pleiades, and move to other planets all the time. With lifetimes that span hundreds of your Earth years, this is a valuable option. Instead of moving to new cities, like you do here on Earth, Pleiadians move to new planets.

"Ah, so this leads to why I am here. Not all planets are easily accessible. Earth is such a planet. It is monitored by the inter-galactic confederation. No one can come here without their approval, with the possible exception of some rogue civilizations, such as Zeta Reticuli, which are not in the confederation. In many ways, I am fortunate to be here. There were many like myself who wanted to come and help with the transition. Only a few thousand were allowed.

"Explaining why I am here is somewhat complicated, especially for your current level of awareness. Let me put it this way: what is happening on Earth at this time will affect all of the planets in the universe — everyone. It is very important for Earth to make this transition in grand style, and I am confident that it will, because there are a lot of souls helping.

"The transition into a new civilization is going to have a very positive impact throughout the universe. What is happening here

Chapter Nine - Dan

on Earth is unique. In many ways, this is a grand experiment. For the first time, a planet of this density is going to evolve in a very short period of time into a highly advanced civilization. Over the next generation, people are going to go from nearly complete ignorance of God to advanced awareness of their divinity. In linear time, it will happen in nearly a snap of the fingers. It is quite amazing what is going to happen in the next thirty years.

"But let me explain what really led me here. We have our problems on Pleiades, just as you have your problems. If this transition goes well, it will help us as much as it will help you."

Teacher squinted his eyes and looked intrigued. "Why?"

"You do not realize it, but the mass consciousness of this planet is creating change. All of you are working together to create this transition. You are showing other civilizations *how* to change. Something incredible is happening here.

"Change is never easy, and is often exceedingly slow and difficult. On Pleiades, it is no different. We change at a snails pace. People accept the status quo. They smile and go about their business. People acknowledge problems, but there is little incentive to promote change. Here on Earth, you are showing us that change is a real possibility."

I laughed. "I just told thousands of people today to sit on their thumbs and *wait* for society to collapse."

Dan looked at me with a straight face. "You advocated change, did you not? You told people to prepare for collapse. What could be a more dire advocating of change?"

I had not considered that perspective. "I suppose you're right."

"Actually, the concept of change is natural here on Earth. That is all you know how to do. You are constantly trying to solve problems or create growth. Instead of accepting the beauty of life, you perceive problems that need to be solved. There is very little satisfaction here, but that is changing. People are now searching for spiritual answers. There is a great urge to find the truth.

"On Pleiades, we have very little desire to change. Most perceive that everything is just fine. For instance, the concept of equality is considered a reality on Pleiades—it is not considered a problem. We perceive that we are equal. But perception is not enough to prevent problems from occurring. For instance, the criteria for making equality a reality is experience. On Pleiades, people still project separation, and many still treat each other as strangers.

"In other words, harmony exists, but it could exist on a much higher level. We could evolve further. And, in order for us to evolve, we must learn to love each other more openly. Here on Earth, you acknowledge problems such as this. You have a myriad of organizations that openly promote change. Earthlings strongly believe that behavior should match your highest values. It is these beliefs that create an impetus for change. But on Pleiades, as strange as this may sound, there are few who believe that anything is wrong. There is already so much harmony that few ever see the need to improve. The very idea of seeking improvement predisposes that a problem exists. Pleiadians prefer to focus on the positive, and ignore anything wrong that exists.

"Does that make sense? In other words, in order to evolve, you must seek evolvement. And on Pleiades, there are few who acknowledge the need for evolvement. Everyone understands that individual growth is why they incarnated. And everyone is seeking growth personally — but not as a group. Group problems are ignored or denied, and this is our illusion. This is what you are going to help us with. By perceiving your illusion, you will help everyone in the universe to perceive theirs.

"It goes something like this. Two Pleiadians will have a conversation:

Chapter Nine - Dan

'The people on Earth sure did change didn't they?'

'It was for the better, wasn't it?'

'Yeah, I'm impressed.'

'So am I.'

'Do you think our planet can change?'

'I don't know? What do you think?'

'Sure, why not, they did. And look at the benefits. They evolved!'

'But aren't we evolving too?'

'It doesn't appear so to me. Nothing seems to change around here. What do you think?'

'Yeah, you're right. But how can we change? How can we evolve?'

'I've got an idea....'

"Conversations like this will start the ball rolling. Eventually, new beliefs will arise and create change throughout the universe. The potential is enormous, and the impetus is right here. This planet is about to set in motion a series of events that will reverberate throughout the cosmos. It is that significant."

He paused.

"That makes sense to me," I said. "The more comfortable you become, the less desire there is for change. Even here in America, there is resistance to change when it's obvious that something is wrong. People love to live in their little bubbles, perceiving everything as just fine. But you're right, change is also natural here."

I continued. "There are always dissatisfied people who desire change. Humans, or Earthlings, as you call us, have always had aspirations to improve things. I suppose it's in our DNA. Here in America, we usually have clear divisions of people on each side of an issue, as people strive to improve the human condition. Thus, change is inevitable and very natural on Earth."

He nodded. "The main reason I am here is because I was frustrated on Pleiades. I am one of those few who advocated change. I felt compelled to come here to help spur change throughout the universe, including on Pleiades. My beliefs led me here. Or, more to the point, my frustrations led me here.

"If you analyze your frustrations, you will understand where your motivation comes from. It is your frustrations that reveal what you need to learn. No one needs anyone to tell them their life goal. All they need to do is analyze their frustrations.

"So, John, what are some of your frustrations?"

"That's easy," I said. "I want to help with the transition. That's all I've wanted since 1989."

"Me, too," Dan said. "Seeing your revolution in the making, I was compelled to help. Both of you were exactly what I was looking for. I felt your intent, and I came to add to your work."

"So our goals are the same?" I asked.

Dan nodded. "Very similar. Although, John, you have other frustrations besides helping humanity during this transition."

He paused.

"I suppose that's true. But what do you see?" I asked, wanting him to explain.

"Mainly, two things. First, you always want to know what is going to happen next in your life. This fear of the unknown frustrates you and leads you to be more controlling in your life than you would prefer to be. Second, not being enlightened frustrates you. This leads to your quest to constantly search for spiritual knowledge."

I smiled. "Amazing. You do know me."

Teacher smiled. "He knows me, too."

"I can help you with your fear of the future," Dan said. "All you need to do is trust that the world is divinely ordered and that your life was pre-planned by *you*. In other words, for *anything*

Chapter Nine - Dan

that happens, you planned for it to happen for a good reason. So, don't try to control the outcome. Instead, embrace whatever comes your way. Trust and love. That is all you need."

"That's beautiful advice," I said. "I will add that to my morning checklist. Okay, I have another question for you, Dan. If I'm searching for spiritual knowledge, then why am I teaching? I've never especially liked teaching. I prefer to be a student."

"You teach because it is what the universe needs, not necessarily what you need. But you also understand that, by teaching others, you are often teaching yourself along the way. A true teacher teaches one on one for long periods of time, and is more concerned with his or her student's progress than his or her own. But, in many respects, teaching others is just a hobby for you."

He was right. I had never felt comfortable teaching one on one, and now I understood why. I was more concerned with my own progress than my student's progress. I was a student, too. Now it was obvious: the reason I taught was so that I could learn, while at the same time helping the universe.

"Thank you, Dan," I said. "You just helped me learn something very important about myself."

He smiled. "You are welcome, John. And don't stop teaching. The universe needs us."

I smiled to acknowledge that I would not stop.

"Dan, is there a particular path to enlightenment? I know that all paths lead to enlightenment, but are there steps that everyone must take? Speaking for myself, I feel as if I need to surrender to God more deeply before I can make additional progress."

He nodded. "First, you must have a complete understanding of yourself and your life purpose. Then you can develop the awareness that everyone is God and everyone is perfect, with their own unique purpose. Only then can you surrender to All That Is, and continue your path to enlightenment.

"Everyone has to go through these steps and surrender to All That Is. The step of surrender is a major step towards enlightenment, and both of you are very close to making it. Both of you are advanced old souls on the precipice of enlightenment. You both have a strong trust in who you are—divinity—but it is still not complete.

"On the one hand, you both know that you are not alone, and you use your guides for assistance. This trust has led you to detach from the external world and rely on the internal. On the other hand, you do not see the divinity in others clearly enough. This lack of awareness comes from a lack of understanding about self, for the self encompasses *everything*. So, as you can see, self is indeed the most important thing to learn. The more you learn about self, the more trust that manifests."

"How can self encompass everything?" I asked.

"You soul does not have a beginning or end. The soul intertwines and interconnects with *all* consciousness. In effect, the soul is connected to everything. You need a bigger view of the self."

"Self encompasses *all*?" I asked.

"Yes," Dan replied. "Just as each cell in your body is unique and distinct, each cell is still part of one body, all consciously connected."

"Each piece of consciousness is not separate from God, but part of God? One *huge* body?" I asked.

"Exactly. And each of us is connected to that huge body."

"Each self is that *huge*?" I asked.

"Exactly. Each self is all-encompassing."

"Then life is a closed system," I said. "One body. One absolute."

Chapter Nine - Dan

"Exactly. From this knowledge, you can trust the perfection of life. For, indeed, there is one absolute, which is perfect. Life truly is divinely ordered."

* * * * *

Dan was a good communicator with great common sense.

Our next conversation dealt with knowledge as the key to spiritual awareness. If you know something, then you believe it, and belief creates reality. For instance, I could say that my life was perfect—divinely ordered—but until I *knew* it, fear would continue to exist in my life. In fact, fear would continue to determine what would occur next.

One tenet of the New Age stated that only the present moment matters, because that is where God exists. It was recommended to spend as little time as possible thinking about the past or the future, and to concern yourself primarily with the present.

Another tenet was that if you want to be happy, then be grateful for the gift of eternal life. If you are grateful enough, then you will be content and happy. A lack of happiness is simply a lack of contentment, arising from the lack of awareness of your eternal soul.

A third tenet was love. Love yourself enough to live a pure life. Love others as you love yourself, out of compassion. And love the planet and all of its life forms out of respect for the creator.

With these three concepts, life could be fulfilling, but such was not the norm. Only a small minority of people had been exposed to these metaphysical concepts. For the vast majority of people, knowledge about self was elusive. People did not believe they created the events in their lives, and lacked the concept of an all encompassing self. They did not believe they were God, or that everyone else was also God.

Once again, it came down to knowledge. Who are you? Who do you believe you are? Most people could never answer this question, and thus could only believe that they didn't know. They could only have belief in doubt. They had no knowledge of who they were, or where they had come from.

Belief is something that we all rely on. One cannot live without believing in something. Most of us believed that we were separate from each other. It was the basis for all our actions. It was the foundation of who we were. It literally created our lives, moment by moment.

* * * * *

"Dan," I said, "talking about beliefs made my mind take off. Are you saying that belief creates intent, and that intent creates our life?"

He grinned. "Yes, exactly. *Your* intent is to add spiritual awareness to the world. You're here to help with the transition, while at the same time increasing your own awareness. You do not yet believe that you are enlightened, so you seek knowledge. Eventually, your level of knowledge will expand, and it will be time to be a true teacher. That is your next step. It is the only way you can prove to yourself that you have learned your lessons."

I smiled. "That makes sense."

Teacher was getting restless. "Are you ready to go?"

I laughed. "Yeah, sure. I didn't realize how long we had been talking."

I remember walking out of the restaurant in a state of wonder. My mind was buzzing. This was the kind of conversation that I really enjoyed.

I spent a lot of time with Dan the following week. We had extraordinary conversations during the day, and then I wrote in my notebook each night.

Chapter Ten

Washington

I arrived back in California refreshed and recharged. My notebook was full, and I would be spending countless hours at the computer. When I was done, I would have a book containing everything that Dan had taught me.

Driving into the condo parking lot, I saw Julie's car parked in our carport. I had not talked to her in a week. I walked into the condo, with a grin on my face, anticipating hugs and kisses. I glanced in the living room. She wasn't there. I went into the kitchen, still no Julie. Next, I checked the bedroom. There she was, changing her clothes and appearing unhappy to see me.

"Hi, hon. How are you doing?" I asked, as I made my way over to her.

"Fine. Good to see you home," she said, with a somber tone and forced smile, as she reached to kiss me.

We hugged and kissed and then she pulled away.

"We have problems," she said, looking concerned.

"Problems? What problems?"

"I'm being followed, and our house is being watched," she said tersely.

"Do you know who it is?" I asked.

"It's the government. It has to be. The cars are unmarked, but they have government plates. The men are clean cut. They wear suits and ties and the same style of sunglasses. I think they're waiting for you."

I was silent.

"Well?" she asked, implying that it was my fault.

Suddenly, someone started knocking on the front door.

"It's them," she said, in a calm voice. "You answer it. John, I don't like this! I prefer a quiet lifestyle." She gave me a strange look.

I started toward the front door. "Julie, everything will calm down. Trust me, it has to. I want a quiet lifestyle, too."

I answered the door. Standing in front of me were two men, dressed in suits and wearing the same wire-rimmed sunglasses. The man closest to the door was holding an ID badge.

"Mr. Randall? We're with the State Department. Can we come in? We need to talk with you."

I studied the ID. "Sure, come in." I opened the door and let them in. They each found a place to sit in the living room. But Julie stayed out of sight.

"Have a seat. Do you mind if I ask why you have been scaring my wife half to death?"

"We didn't mean to cause any inconvenience. We were waiting for you. Just doing our job. Sorry if we caused any problems."

"You could have given my wife your number and had me call you when I got home. There's no reason for the cloak and dagger routine."

"We're sorry, but there's no time. Our orders were to find you ASAP. We need you to come to Washington immediately. In fact, we need you to start packing right now."

I laughed nervously. "You're serious? Do I have a choice?"

Chapter Ten - Washington

"As soon as you're packed, we will head for the airport. We'll talk on the plane, although there's not much that we can tell you. And no, you don't have a choice."

I hesitated.

"This is a highly unusual situation," he continued empathetically. "Please don't make us do it the hard way. You will be on that plane in thirty minutes. And don't expect explanations, because we don't have any. This is top secret. All we know is that you are to be brought to Washington ASAP for a meeting. Let us do our job in a non-confrontational manner."

"Am I or my wife in any danger? When will I be brought home?"

"I'm sorry, I don't have those answers. We're wasting time. Do you pack, or do we pack for you?" He raised his eyebrows.

I was confused, but I had no reason to be afraid. The answers to my questions were most likely in Washington. "I'll pack. I just thought I would ask. Give me five minutes, and we'll be out of here."

When I walked into the bedroom to pack, Julie was waiting for me.

"I have to go with them to Washington for a meeting," I said.

"I know, I was listening." She paused. "I'll be waiting for you, but this can not continue." The stress in her voice was evident.

"It won't," I replied, not sure if I could keep that promise. After all, recent events seemed to be out of my hands.

After packing, I gave Julie a hug and kiss. "I'm not sure when I'll be home," I said. "I'll call you when I can."

She nodded, with tears in her eyes.

I sat in the back seat, and they sat in the front. The driver drove as if he was in a hurry. An identical, black Ford Lincoln followed. My mind was racing with thoughts. I was wishing I'd had more time to talk with Julie. She was clearly frustrated.

I don't think these last few months were what she had in mind when she married me. In fact, I had the unpleasant feeling that she might not put up with this much longer.

I thought about asking questions, but then thought better of it. Until we boarded the plane, I decided to keep my mouth shut. The better the relationship I had with these agents, the more information I might obtain — if they had any to give.

Both cars drove at high speeds, south on Interstate 5, to El Toro Air Force Base. We drove through a security gate without stopping, and parked next to a waiting Gulfstream jet with its engines running. Quickly, we exited the car, climbed the boarding stairs, and found our seats. Within seconds, the airplane door was closed and we were in the air. It had been less than thirty minutes since I had arrived home from Santa Fe. The roller coaster continued.

I was sitting near the middle of the plane, next to one of my escorts, an older man who obviously was the higher ranking agent. The other agent was sitting a few rows behind us.

"Mr. Randall...," he started.

"John," I interrupted. "Call me John."

"Okay, John," he continued. "I don't know why they want you in Washington. All I can tell you is that it has something to do with the war, and that your help is required. You are not under arrest or anything like that. Your assistance is required, that is all." He paused and said sincerely, "You probably know more about this than we do."

"Yeah, I have an idea. I met with the Underground three months ago in Ireland. I'm sure this is related."

He raised his eyebrows and looked at me seriously. "What were you doing in Europe, meeting with the Underground?"

I hesitated. "If you haven't been told, are you supposed to ask that question? I mean, aren't you guys just delivering me?"

Chapter Ten - Washington

"You're probably right, but I'm curious. You can tell me."

I grinned. "So what's your name?"

"Dave," he replied.

"So, Dave, how curious are you? Do you want to hear about the meeting?"

"Sure. Who else is going to know? There's no one else here except the pilots, and they can't hear us."

"Okay, then. We have a five-hour flight ahead of us," I said. "Do you want to get your partner up here, because he won't believe you when you repeat it."

"Hey, Jeff, come and join us."

Jeff made his way towards us and sat in the opposite aisle.

"I was going to tell Dave why I think I'm on this plane. Are you interested?" I asked.

He nodded. Jeff appeared to be in his twenties, maybe even new to government service. I suspected that he might be a young soul, but didn't want to exclude him, if he wanted to join in our conversation.

"Okay. I'm glad we have five hours; we might need it. Where do I begin? How about 1989? That's a good starting point. That's when I learned about metaphysics and the future."

I paused and looked at each of them in turn. Neither reacted, but I had their attention.

I continued. "At the time, I was a relatively normal person like yourselves, as far as beliefs go. For instance, I believed that God was separate from me and resided in heaven. I believed that Jesus died for our sins and was the only son of God. However, I was different than most in one way. I was a covert radical. I refused to join any organizations. The thought of joining society was repulsive to me. Something didn't feel right about it, almost to the point where it felt like society and civilization were corrupt.

"As a result, I thought my life was going to be a long, difficult struggle of pointlessness. I didn't know what I was looking for, but I was looking for something that gave me peace of mind. I was definitely searching. I knew there had to be more, but I had no idea what it was.

"I wasn't searching in any specific way, because I didn't know what to look for, or if there was even anything to find. I thought that what we were exposed to was all there was—that there were no secrets.

"Then in 1989, my world view changed. I was introduced to reality—metaphysics. Not the reality you perceive, but a *new* reality. In essence, I found what I was looking for.

"I remember it well. I was sitting on the edge of my bed at two in the morning, listening intently to the radio, knowing that what I was hearing would change my life forever. It was as if the radio guest were jogging some deep soul memory. I was remembering who I was and why I was here. This was the key that would lead me to all of the answers I sought. It was the epiphany I didn't expect, yet always hoped for.

"As I sat on the edge of my bed, I felt a feeling that I had never felt before. I felt a connection with another consciousness, a *oneness* with humanity. I knew, in that instance, that all consciousness was connected, and that my soul was the link. Later, when I read that we are all connected, it made sense to me because I had already experienced it.

"I didn't feel alone, listening to the radio that night. There was another consciousness connected to me. That is the only way I can describe it. It was as if a consciousness had come to join me. It was a loving consciousness that came to give me a message: *This is what you have been looking for. Listen carefully.* The consciousness came with a feeling that I will never forget. I can't explain it with words. It's a feeling that transcends words, but it was *real*.

Chapter Ten - Washington

"I have never felt alone, since. I can't tell you that you aren't alone, because you have to feel it for yourself. Your awareness has to feel the connection to others. You have to remember that you are one with everything...."

Jeff was steadily getting uncomfortable, and could no longer keep quiet. "You are one of those New Age people, aren't you? With all those crazy beliefs? You people really disturb me. What you believe goes against everything I have been taught in my life.

"You can listen to him, but I've had enough," Jeff fumed, and headed toward the back of the plane.

Dave shook his head at his young associate's outburst. "Jeff isn't too hip to the New Age movement. He thinks you're all wacko." He laughed, but then looked at me intently. "So, who was that radio guest and what did they say that helped you to remember oneness?"

"The guest was Dolores Cannon. She does hypnotic regression. This is when you hypnotize someone and bring the person to a past life. On this show, she was publicizing a book titled *Conversations with Nostradamus*. She had made contact with Nostradamus — the man who could see the future. She was describing things in the future that Nostradamus told her about. I knew she had made contact with him, and somehow this had awakened my memory. Suddenly I *knew* that this was the key to my life. This was what I had been looking for.

"Nostradamus told Dolores possible futures. He could see many, and told her the bad ones. His goal was to try to prevent atrocities by exposing us to what *could* happen. He believed that, if we saw it coming, we could select a better future. Dolores transcribed his words into a book — three volumes, actually. He described the fall of the Berlin wall; the splitting up of the Soviet Union; natural disasters and Earth changes; the dissolution of the Catholic Church, including the last three Popes; and the rise of an

Arab leader in the Middle East who would attempt to take over the world.

"What he said about spirituality is what changed me. He said that religions would soon dissolve and that the next civilization would be based on the spirituality of the New Age movement. *That* got my attention. I considered myself a Christian, but I had always believed something was lacking with Christianity—that it was flawed. For, how else could you define the Crusades or the Inquisition? I wasn't comfortable belonging to any organized Christian religion, for this reason. I considered Jesus a messiah, but not the only way to heaven. I also believed his message of compassion and love was largely ignored by Christian religions. He taught compassion and love, not morality and judgment.

"So, after that night, I started reading New Age literature. It was all I read for a decade. I read book after book. I was completely amazed by what I learned. I had no idea that such knowledge existed. After a few years, I had educated myself. I learned a new perception of reality. I learned who I am, or more precisely, who *we* are—a divine oneness.

"Steadily my spirituality began to overwhelm my life. First I began writing about spirituality; then I began teaching. Today, I have an enlightenment school. I focus my life on learning about spirituality and metaphysics and exposing others to what I know.

"I can explain the dynamics of life, of which few are aware. For instance, this war is meaningless. It doesn't matter who wins, because the world is going to soon change into a new civilization. The war will end soon, and the world will begin to transform. Many times, I have asked myself why I know what I know. I think it is because some people must show the way.

I paused. "I suppose I should tell you about some of the knowledge I have learned. First, we are God, or more specifically, aspects of God. There is no separation between us and God. For, everything is *one* and everything is connected by consciousness. You are no more separate from God than your fingers are separate from your hand. The same consciousness that connects your fingers, connects you to God. God is a fragmented whole, much like your fingers are fragments of your body. If anything happens to one of your fingers, the rest of your body *knows* about it.

"In essence, God is the consciousness of All That Is. God is the integrated whole. In short, God is not a being that judges us. God is a consciousness that interacts with us. God is intricately a part of us, and we are intricately a part of God. This is complicated to explain with words, because God cannot be known with words or the intellect."

"Fascinating concept," Dave said. "God is *all*. I never thought of God like that before." He hesitated in contemplation. "If that concept was accepted, it could transform the whole world...."

He looked stunned. "My God, is that why you're on this plane?"

I smiled. "Exactly. Enough of the sermon. You're probably wondering how I know this, yet you've never heard of it. I wondered the same thing. I used to shake my head in wonder. How could the truth that we are all God be hidden? How come nobody has released it to the public? How could it be kept a secret?"

He nodded, wanting the answer.

"It's complicated. It turns out that because we're all connected by consciousness, we create an integrated mass consciousness. This mass consciousness creates our experiences and is dictated by our beliefs. Today, because the vast majority believe we are separate from God, this concept of oneness is not easily transmitted to the masses. In effect, the masses don't want to hear it. This desire of not wanting to hear it is actually part of the mass consciousness. Thus, the mass consciousness blocks this from happening on a mass scale. However, each individual is free to find this truth, and as people do find it, this steadily impacts the mass consciousness."

"That makes sense," Dave said. "It's kind of like a new medication or invention. Initially, a few brave souls have to try it before it will catch on. Thus, this block will eventually lift and the mass consciousness will come to accept this concept of oneness."

I nodded, surprised by his quick grasp of the truth. "This truth that we are God and all one is slowly being accepted. Eventually, it will be dispersed to the masses and the world will change. Until then, it will steadily be exposed to more individuals, such as yourself. Moreover, only those with ears to hear will grasp it. In other words, you must be ready, or else this knowledge will make little sense."

"What do you mean by ready?" Dave asked.

"I'll give you the short version. Each of us has incarnated many times. These incarnations allow our souls to evolve and to steadily become more aware of our divinity. This awareness eventually increases until we are enlightened, or completely aware of our divinity. Those who have evolved to a certain degree of awareness in previous lifetimes are ready to accept the concept of oneness."

"I think I understand," Dave said. "With each lifetime, our awareness of our divinity increases. Eventually, this leads to enlightenment."

I nodded. "Exactly. What is about to happen—is happening—is that this planet is about to transform into a new civilization that is enlightened. Conversely, the current civilization is about to disappear. The new one will be aware of the oneness of life. What is about to happen is an incredible event in the history of this planet."

Chapter Ten - Washington

"Unbelievable," Dave said, trying to picture this dazzling future.

"Almost," I said. "If oneness were not a reality, then it would be unbelievable. However, oneness is *real*. What will happen is an awakening, a remembering."

"Wow," Dave said, fascinated.

"Let me answer some of your questions about why I'm on this plane and why I had contact with the Underground. One of my former students joined the Underground several years ago, and came in contact with the Underground leader. He talks a lot, and he tells everyone he meets about the New Age movement in America.

"The leader became very interested in the movement, and tried to get more information. However, that is nearly impossible with the war. As you know, nothing gets in or out of Europe. But the leader was curious, and thought perhaps he could learn something from his friend's teacher....

"So, three months ago, I went to Ireland to explain what the New Age movement was all about. Some close friends of mine had asked me to go, and I agreed. I don't really know why I went, other than as a favor to them.

"When I got there, I discovered that the Underground leader had actually contacted the U. S. government and requested me by name. I did not actually meet him, but they recorded my message, and I'm sure he heard it.

"After I returned from the meeting in Ireland, it was announced by the U.S. government that the New Age movement was the panacea for all of our national problems. Shortly after that announcement, I was named one of the New Age leaders, just because of that meeting.

"Then last week, I gave a speech at the New Age political convention that was televised to twenty million people. And now, you show up at my door.

"I'm on this airplane because the New Age is *real*, and it's going to begin soon. Events are transpiring to put everything in motion. Belief systems are about to re-align."

"You mean an awakening is occurring?" Dave asked in disbelief.

I nodded. "Yes, although the government doesn't believe it. They're still trying to win the war and revert to our previous way of life. That's what this plane trip is all about. The government wants to work with the Underground to win the war, and they think that I'm their only link. It's kind of ironic, since I'm anti-war and basically anti-government."

I laughed. "The government doesn't even care what I know about spirituality. They probably won't even ask me, and I won't offer anything. What's about to transpire — if I'm right — is predictable. They're going to ask me to help them make contact with the Underground.

"They don't care one bit about the New Age movement. Even if the Underground leader is interested, they could not care less. And it's the knowledge of this movement that they should be seeking and trying to understand. So be it."

"Why *don't* they care?" Dave asked.

"Because it doesn't fit into their mindset. Belief systems dictate behavior, and the current belief systems of the military are not ready for New Age thought. For instance, you can't very well kill your enemy, if you perceive that he is you."

"No, I guess not!" Dave shook his head in understanding.

"So," I continued, "I'll play their game and see how it plays out. What choice do I have?"

Chapter Ten - Washington

I paused. "That's about it. Now you can ask questions, and I'll try my best to answer."

He nodded. "Okay, let me see if I can understand what you have been saying. This whole war is meaningless because of the spiritual changes that are about to occur. The Underground leader is beginning to understand this, and so he wants to learn more. He wants to find out if this could be true. Then there's our side. The government wants to win the war and doesn't care about the New Age movement."

He paused.

I grinned and nodded. "Keep going, you're doing great."

"You haven't told me much about yourself," he continued, "but from what you have said, I gather you understand life more clearly than the rest of us. And that the average citizen, such as myself, doesn't have a clue about the reality of life."

"Something like that," I said. "Continue."

"So, a New Age is upon us, and people like you are preparing the way. You're giving people like me hints about what is to come, in very subtle ways. Subtle, because the masses are not yet ready for the truth. You can't just come out and tell everyone that they're God. The masses are not ready to comprehend that yet."

"Yes, that's correct. Continue."

"So, there's a preparation going on for this New Age. Information is slowly seeping into the masses, as people like you release it in small doses. More and more, people are remembering that they are part of a whole — a oneness.

"There is an inevitability about this awakening, because what you are espousing is the truth. Thus, people are steadily awakened, and the movement grows. I guess people such as you are modern-day apostles. You're spreading the word."

I grimaced. "I don't consider myself an evangelist who is spreading dogma. Sometimes I wish that I wasn't even a writer and teacher. I don't want to push beliefs upon people—just expose people to new ideas."

Dave laughed. "I wouldn't call expounding an awareness of our inherent divinity a new idea. You're spreading gospel, my friend."

I didn't reply, and he continued. "The leader of the Underground learns about the movement from one of your students and thinks there must be something to all this. Is that what this is all about? The leader has found God?"

I shrugged. "Maybe, or possibly he just wants to understand what the movement's about."

He paused in contemplation. "Do you have any proof or anything tangible to prove that we are God?"

"No, only a personal knowing that came to me through experience. I cannot prove to you the existence of God, especially not with words. You have to find God for yourself. Reading can often awaken something within. I would recommend reading metaphysical material and see what happens. There are many sources, such as Seth from the 1960s, Michael from the 1970s, and an abundance of sources from the 1980s and onward. If these sources don't awaken you to the existence of God, then you're probably not ready."

I paused. "Could these sources lead us astray? I suppose it's a possibility, but that doesn't ring true in my heart. After reading as many sources as I have, the only conclusion I have drawn is that the truth is being revealed. The New Age is almost upon us."

"So what do we do? What do you recommend?" he asked.

"For yourself, I would recommend that you learn how to follow your heart. Don't let anyone influence you. Find your own truth and guide yourself from within."

I pointed to my heart. "Not from your head, but from your heart."

Chapter Ten - Washington

He suddenly appeared solemn and contemplative. "That's good advice," he said. "I might even read a New Age book."

I smiled.

Chapter 11

Ogmios

As we got off the plane, two men in military fatigues and black boots were waiting for us. They didn't smile when they told me to get in the back seat of the vehicle. I followed orders and kept my mouth shut. Both military men got in the back seat with me, one on each side. Another military man was already in the driver's seat. Dave and Jeff remained behind.

I thought that we might be going to the Pentagon, but we got off the highway and were now driving in the country. After a short drive, we turned off the road and approached a large security gate. Then, to my amazement, we were driving underground, on a paved road in a lighted tunnel. We were going to an underground base.

We approached what I can only describe as an underground city. It was huge inside and extremely well lit. The ceilings were three stories high as far as the eye could see, with many single story buildings covering dozens of acres. Thousands of people could live here, I thought. We parked near the entrance and switched to a small electric vehicle. There was a flurry of activity, with dozens of these electric vehicles swarming around. Everyone was wearing a military uniform of one type or another.

We drove to a group of buildings, and I was ushered into a meeting room. When I walked into the room, I was stunned. Very few times in recent years had I lost my composure, but I was quite nervous. There, sitting right in front of me, was Ogmios himself—the leader of the Underground! I couldn't believe it. What was he doing here?

I recognized his face from some obscure news clippings that I had come across, even though he was only mentioned by one mysterious code name or another. I wondered, briefly, if the AC had ever seen his picture or knew his actual identity. But on this grand occasion, I was too polite to pose such questions.

We were left alone. He was seated in a chair behind a plain table. On the table were a notepad and pen, along with a tape recorder. There were no windows or any other furniture except another chair opposite his. It was a small meeting room. As I approached the table, he arose with an authentic grin, extending his hand in friendship.

"Hello, John" he said, in a deep, eastern European accent. "Thank you for coming."

He wore a military uniform, although it was clean and he was well groomed. For a military man, he appeared to be very cordial and friendly. He was in his 60s, and had a twinkle in his eye that made you feel comfortable in his presence. I suspected that his charisma contributed strongly to his ability to lead and command respect.

I shook his hand. "It's a pleasure to meet you," I said sincerely, with profound respect.

"You know who I am, don't you?" he asked politely, sitting back down.

"I can't believe it, but I think you're Ogmios," I replied, finding my seat.

"Ogmios? Who is Ogmios?" he asked, seriously.

"Ogmios is the name that Nostradamus gave to the leader of the Underground. The name Ogmios represents something in Greek history. I'm not sure what it means, but that doesn't

Chapter 11 - Ogmios

matter. If you're Ogmios, and I think you are, it's a rare privilege to meet you."

He obviously found this amusing. "Well, I am Greek!" he laughed. "And if you want to call me Ogmios, that is okay with me," he said in a firm, yet friendly, tone. "Yes, I am the leader of the Underground. I'm here today because I listened to the tape you made for me in Ireland, and I wanted to meet you. I thought about meeting you in Europe, but this was much safer and easier. The U.S. government has been begging me to communicate with them. So I decided to accomplish two things at once."

He appeared to be reading my body language. And it was obvious that I was not to learn his real name.

"Why did you want to meet me?" I asked, completely confused.

He grinned, and answered straightforwardly. "I need your help. I'm trying to spread your New Age knowledge. More precisely, I'm trying to spread your knowledge to the power brokers of the world, who make decisions about people's lives."

Now he had my full attention. My facial expression was that of astonishment and wonder.

He continued. "We're going to educate some very important people. I know about the New Age movement and I think it's the future. Otherwise, I wouldn't be here today. That first tape you made in Ireland wasn't only for me. It was also for the U.S. military and the power brokers who give them orders. With your help, I'm going to educate them all. Do you approve?" he asked, grinning.

"Wow, this is fascinating." I nodded. "What do you want me to do?"

He smiled. "I thought that you would understand. But, before we begin, do you have any specific questions?"

I reflected for a moment. "Did you have anything to do with the New Age movement being recognized by the U.S. government?"

He nodded. "I twisted some arms. Actually, I think they have been considering its inevitability for a long time."

"So it was you who made me a household name?"

"You could say that," he said matter-of-factly. "You were chosen after a careful selection process. I spied on you and many of your friends, and then I picked you. It was your destiny, my friend."

I nodded, instantly forgiving him.

Despite his age, Ogmios had a youthful appearance. I could tell he was tired and had been working hard. He appeared, however, in control, and his leadership qualities were becoming more and more apparent. He seemed highly intelligent, quick witted, and projected an air of strength. He was no-nonsense, yet easy-going and sincere at the same time. It was an unusual combination, and you almost *had to* like him.

He grinned warmly. "Okay, to business. Your first tape was helpful. People in high places listened to it. This will be your second, and even more people will listen — considering where it was made and that I was in the room." He lifted his eyebrows and grinned impishly at his fiendishly clever plan.

"Before we begin," I said, "I have another question. Will I be able to return to my normal life after this meeting? The last three months have been a bit of a ride. I would like to go back to a reasonable life. My wife is getting a bit edgy, and I think she might just leave me, if this continues."

He reflected for a second, then quickly commented. "I'll call off the dogs for a while. At least for a year, that is. I cannot promise you more than that. I might need your help in the future." He suddenly had that serious look again.

Chapter 11 - Ogmios

I nodded. I was not about to tell this man no. I was relieved that I would have the chance to relax for a year.

He continued to brief me. "You have to explain to them why this war is not as important as the coming spiritual revolution. They really don't care what you have to say, but I still want to tell them. The powers that be are focusing all of their energy on winning this war against the antichrist. As we both know, they are missing the point."

"Is this why you have refused to have any cooperation with the U.S. government? Different objectives?" I asked curiously.

He nodded. "That's correct. I'll have nothing to do with them. My army is all that I need. We have no allies except God, and God is a great ally."

I smiled. "Indeed. You must be driving them crazy with your intransigence."

"Do I care?" he said jokingly. "I don't need them. The AC doesn't have a chance of winning."

"All right, I'm ready to speak," I said.

He turned on the tape recorder, and then pushed it toward me.

"John Randall, I would like you to tell me about the war, from your perspective."

I contemplated. "The best place to begin this discussion is with the concept of evil, because that is how the enemy has been defined. Society's current belief system accepts the notion of good and evil. However, there is no such thing as evil, as defined as separate from God...."

Ogmios interrupted. "You realize that many would say it is imperative to combat the atrocities of this war?"

"Of course," I replied. "But the truth is that there is no such thing as evil. Why? Because each of us is God. Life exists as a oneness of consciousness. Nothing can exist outside of God's domain. And because God is perfection, so is life on Earth. It is impossible for evil, as a separate force, and perfection to coexist. Simply put, evil is an illusion, as is morality.

"Morality is nothing more than society's attempt at defining how people should live, using subjective ideas of right and wrong. This is why morality constantly changes from generation to generation. Morals are based on ideas that we currently have, often an interpretation of how we think God wants us to live.

"As much as people would like to believe that God agrees with their morality, it simply isn't so. God agrees with no one, because morality can never be absolute. God perceives our morality as ours, not God's. God uses karma to define right and wrong, not morality. Thus, God doesn't sentence us to hell for our behavior, but instead gives us new lives, so that we can learn from our mistakes. God is compassionate, has infinite patience, and is not concerned with justice or discipline.

"When someone hurts or kills a fellow human being, they are simply hurting or killing themselves. God understands this. What that soul needs is not to be punished, but to be given the opportunity to evolve to the point where they understand that such behavior makes no sense.

"We have all likely murdered someone in a previous life, but that doesn't make us evil. When we define the enemy as evil, we are being ignorant of their inherent divinity. We don't want to condone murder, but we should be compassionate, loving, and patient—like God. Their karma is to come later. No one gets away with anything, and everyone must learn their lessons, which are not always easy."

"Wait," Ogmios said. "I'm confused. If God is perfection, and we are God, why would we create karma that needs to be resolved? Wouldn't our behaviors always be perfect?"

Chapter 11 - Ogmios

"This is where it gets confusing, and our human minds have trouble understanding. For, although life is perfection, our souls often use negative behavior to evolve. In fact, that is the purpose of life—the evolution of the soul. Our objective is to become like God, with God's qualities of compassion, unconditional love, and infinite patience. And the best way to learn these values is to experience the opposite. Just as we learned that light is the absence of darkness, we can learn to choose love over fear, forgiveness over revenge, and so on.

"God knows that we are going to have difficulty learning these values, so this is where karma comes into play. Each time we try to learn using negative behavior, we create karma. This karma accumulates, and we must experience behaviors that resolve the karma. Our karma literally directs and dictates our life experiences."

Ogmios nodded, accepting my answer.

"This doesn't mean that we should legalize murder and rape and then expect God to apply justice using karma. We don't want to commit these negative behaviors, and we don't want to encourage them. But we should still be more compassionate to offenders. For instance, the death penalty shouldn't be used.

"I should probably explain evil a little bit more. There is only one force in the universe, and that force is God. There is no duality of forces that oppose each other. Yes, there are positive and negative, but these forces are actually one and the same. They don't really oppose each other."

"You are implying," Ogmios said, "that God uses the negative to learn. That God uses the negative to learn the positive. You are actually saying that the negative is not necessarily a bad thing. That it is literally useful."

"Yes," I nodded. "There is nothing right or wrong about any experience. There are extremes on this planet that we loathe, but they create experiences that are useful for the soul. To experience the negative is quite natural for the soul. Negativity is chosen to learn from, and chosen in a positive sense. Everyone chooses it, in one form or another. Like I said, it is natural.

"What must be understood is that, after the soul evolves to a certain point, the negative is no longer desired. In fact, after enough negativity has been experienced, the soul steadily seeks out love and avoids negativity. This is how life works, and it is a slow process that requires many, many lifetimes."

Ogmios raised his eyebrows. "From a reincarnation standpoint, I can understand that."

"Reincarnation is a reality," I continued, "and lives are spent experiencing degrees of positive and negative. This planet shields us from our true selves and provides an excellent opportunity for learning. We choose to incarnate here, knowing that we'll be limited in our awareness of reality. We arrive here, not knowing who we are or where we came from. In essence, we use this ignorance to learn lessons and expand our awareness."

I paused to let my words register for a moment, then went on. "We learn from our experiences, be they positive or negative. Thus, all experiences are valid. We are part of God, and God's objective is to experience the infinite...."

Ogmios whistled. "That's quite a statement. You're implying that God *wants* to experience the negative."

I nodded. "Life is perfection. So nothing can ever occur without God's blessing. In fact, our lives are pre-planned. Before we incarnate, we know exactly what our potential experiences will entail."

"I have another question," Ogmios said. "If God is not a being, then how can God bless something?"

I grinned. "You are right; God does not exist as an individual being. God exists as the *whole*. God is aware of all consciousness and can influence any piece of that consciousness. You have to think really *big*. Our individual consciousness is not separate from God, but connected. God knows our choices and how they will impact other people's choices. God is like a huge computer that keeps everything in harmony. In fact, God is always three steps ahead of everyone, anticipating what is going to happen, according to our choices."

Ogmios was astonished. "Wow, if that's true, that is incredible!"

"We are eternal, and our awareness is constantly expanding. God has infinite patience with our choices, and we have infinite time to reach our destiny—enlightenment. God loves us unconditionally. God has to, because we are part of God."

"How does this lesson on evil have anything to do with the war?" Ogmios asked.

"Well, if evil is part of God, then there is no reason to resist it. Even the Bible states this, 'Resist not evil.' In other words, let those who want to fight a war do it on their own. Let it be their experience, but not yours.

"It's not evil that created the war, but a false belief in evil. Belief in evil set in motion a series of events that led to this war. The antecedents of this war actually go back many generations, all of which have had the same belief system.

"Many, today, blame the AC—the antichrist—for the war. Wrong. The AC is merely playing a role, created by the current belief system. The AC is not an inherently evil man. He is simply a soul who accepted the challenge of experiencing extreme negativity. The AC is a part of God, just like you and me. We are as much the AC, as the AC himself. He is our brother, as is everyone else.

"I need to add some greater explanation here. Events that we experience are put in motion by our beliefs. Nothing happens by accident, and everything is based on belief. Beliefs are always manifested in the future as experience. What we believe today will manifest sometime in the future. In other words, beliefs of the past put this war in motion, and beliefs that we currently hold sustain it.

"Everything is much more ordered than we perceive. As I just stated, we manifest what we *believe*. The war was manifested by all of us. Thus, we created it together. However, just as we created it, we can end it. In fact, that is what is happening...."

"What do you mean?" Ogmios asked, intrigued.

"This civilization is coming to an end. We are in the beginning of a transition into a new civilization. This war is part of that transition. It is the last war, and it is teaching us that war solves nothing.

"Let me explain why a new civilization is being born. God is harmony, and when there is too much disharmony, there is always decay and eventually a collapse. This is why civilizations come to an end. Our civilization is in extreme disharmony today, and it is steadily destroying the planet. Before the planet is destroyed, however, God is going to end our civilization and start over."

Ogmios looked at me intently. "Does the outcome of the war impact the birth of this new civilization?"

"No. It's the other way around. The new civilization will end the war. The belief systems are going to change so radically that no one will want to fight. Everything will change. Civilization will become love based, and war will be no more."

Ogmios laughed. "No more war? You've got to be kidding."

"I'm not," I said seriously. "Civilization is soon going to start over with new beliefs. We will no longer believe in separation from God — or in separation from each other. We will believe in our divinity and our eternalness. We will believe that everything

Chapter 11 - Ogmios

is *one* and *all* humans are as special as every other human being. From this viewpoint, war will be viewed as irrational and a waste of life. Soon, people will come to regard life as precious, and each person as sovereign. Killing another human being will no longer be viewed as something that is acceptable."

Ogmios whistled again. "That's what the New Age movement is trying to instill? These new beliefs?"

I nodded. "Yes. It's happening."

"Okay," Ogmios said, "let's move to another question. Why do you believe this?"

I hesitated. "Let's start with Nostradamus. His record speaks for itself. He clearly foresaw Napoleon and Hitler. He also accurately predicted the fall of the Catholic Church, with only two Popes following John Paul II. Next, he predicted the rise of the AC, whom he called the man in the blue turban. He also correctly predicted that the world economy would collapse during these end times. It is evident that he saw the future.

"His predictions of the AC were elaborate. He described how the AC's humanitarian efforts would entice the world. That he would slowly build his power base, using a communications network and a web of economic links. Then, before anyone could stop him, he would plunge upon Greece and Turkey, and then fiercely attack Italy. Europe would be engulfed in war before anyone knew what the AC was up to.

"Perhaps the most significant Nostradamus prediction was that the war would end in 2029, when the continents would shift and large portions of the land mass would be submerged by the ocean. And that the survivors would use the New Age movement as the basis for the next civilization. He went even further. He explained how the next civilization would live during the Age of Aquarius. People would learn to love each other. Everyone would view each other as related, and spirituality would blossom.

"It is significant what Nostradamus said. He said that there would no longer be organized religion and that the New Age movement would represent individual spirituality. The New Age is about each individual finding his or her own truth, his or her own spirituality. The group religions of our current civilization are about conformity and pushing views on others. The next civilization will understand the flaw in group religion, which is predicated upon dogma. A relationship with God cannot be shared with others. It is between God and ourselves. It is an individual experience, a Gnostic experience.

"Nostradamus' message of the future is about love. He is trying to guide us towards the New Age, a new civilization. He said that love is ahead and to get ready for it. His message of reincarnation implies that there is nothing to be afraid of ... and he taught us much more.

"Nostradamus is a good starting point, but there are many other sources that verify his vision. The amount of material that has come from the other side since 1960 is astounding: Jane Roberts (Seth), Jani King (P'Taah), Barbara Marciniak (The Pleiadians), Lee Carroll (Kryon), Neal Donald Walsch (God), Mary-Margaret Moore (Bartholomew), Michael Newton (hypnotic regression), Pepper Lewis (Gaia), and Dolores Cannon (hypnotic regression).

"This material is all correlative. The key elements in the material are the oneness of life, reincarnation, and the coming Earth changes. These concepts have been denied extensively by the powers that be and the mainstream media, as well as most organized religions.

"Once reincarnation and oneness are recognized by the majority, that will change everything. No longer will good and evil be easily definable. No longer will social status and identity be important. Everything will change. For instance, reincarnation implies that everyone experiences *everything*. Thus, judgment becomes moot, or, at the very least, redefined."

"Are you saying," Ogmios said, "that this recognition is coming soon? And that once it comes, the outcome of the war will be moot?"

I nodded. "That's exactly what I am saying. This war is nothing but the last lesson of war. In fact, this particular war is an experience with no winner. Thus, the basis for winning the war is irrelevant. We have already decided, on a mass consciousness level, to start a new civilization. Once the new civilization begins to dawn, the war will end."

"A new civilization?" Ogmios said.

I nodded. "Yes. One could say that God has had enough. Look at the hatred and prejudice that exists around the world. We have religious wars, race wars, cultural wars, resource wars. How many people were killed last year at the hands of fellow humans? Not to mention the very subtle discrimination that is pervasive between diverse social groups. It is evident that civilization is not getting better. God has decided to start over. Our time is up.

"As a civilization, the decision was made to have one last major war before the transition. We've been a war-based civilization, so we might as well go out with a war."

"How did civilization decide?" Ogmios asked.

"Our planet has a mass consciousness, and everyone's beliefs add to this consciousness. Decisions of this magnitude are made by the combined thoughts of everyone. It's like a giant computer that God uses. We made the decision to have one more war, but it is a war with no outcome. The AC can do what he wants to win this war, but the outcome has already been decided. We shall start over."

"Okay, let's go on to the next question," Ogmios said. "Why is Christianity on the wane in America? What's happening to organized religion?"

"It's coming to an end. Why? Because it's based on a false foundation. The belief that God is a judgmental being and is separate from us is false. People are beginning to recognize this false foundation. This is why the New Age movement is expanding.

"Jesus' message was supposed to be the basis for Christianity, but that has not been the case. Jesus said to spread the word that God loves everyone equally. Somehow, however, that message got lost. Instead, we created a religion where only *believers* go to heaven. People refused to accept that message of unconditional love and a non-judgmental God. They much preferred the message of the Old Testament, "Live in fear of God."

"The New Age movement is about bringing Jesus' message back: God loves everyone equally and *without* judgment. God loves everyone equally, because we *are* God. When Jesus said that the Kingdom of God is in your heart, he meant that God is part of us. Moreover, if God is part of us, then there is no need to be saved. Jesus tried to get people to acknowledge God within. And Mary Magdalene's gospel clearly states that God can be found within. That is a common message of the New Age movement. Everyone can have a personal relationship with God.

"Christianity focuses on God's judgment of sin. Jesus tried to expose this fallacy by keeping company with so-called sinners. He didn't try to save them from hell. In his eyes, they were his equal, as all people are equal. Today, however, Christians want to punish sinners. Something became lost in Jesus' humanitarian teachings.

"People today are rebelling against the moral judgments from the religious communities. Gays and other diverse groups

Chapter 11 - Ogmios

are tired of being told that God rejects their beliefs and lifestyles. There has been too much focus on good and evil and what God wants. Conversely, there has not been a correlative amount of compassion, understanding, and patience. Instead, the fear of God has created an obsession with morality. People are living in fear of God's judgment, which doesn't even exist."

"That's quite a statement," Ogmios said.

"Most old souls recognize the faulty belief system of Christianity. The belief system that Jesus' spoke of has been lost. Today, in its place, is a system of belief that has led to separation, conflict, division, guilt, and fear. The result is that humanity has been split apart in conflict. For humanity to come together in harmony, a new belief system must arise—one that recognizes the fallacy of separation and death."

I stopped.

"I agree with you," Ogmios said, "that humanity is split apart and in conflict. But I can't see people changing their beliefs. How can that happen?"

"Have you heard of the hundredth-monkey theory?"

"Yeah," Ogmios replied. "Once a new behavior is started by a certain number of monkeys, it will affect all monkeys—even if they live in different countries."

I nodded. "Once a small percentage of the world's population recognizes that they are God, the rest will follow. We are quickly approaching this point. Once we reach critical mass, it will only take a few years for this new belief to be accepted by 25% of the world's population. In a decade, it will be accepted by over 50%. And then by 2050, nearly everyone will believe it."

Ogmios was shocked. "You're serious? We're that close?"

I nodded. "Yes. It's going to happen."

I paused, but Ogmios didn't respond.

"At a time when the world needs to come together, Christians have plotted ways to fight evil. In their eyes, the problem is evil, and evil is bad. This is a faulty belief system. And as I've said previously, belief creates experience. This is why we have conflict throughout the world."

I stopped and looked at Ogmios.

"One last question," he said. "If everything is perfect, how can you explain the violence and suffering that people are being exposed to?"

I laughed. "You could at least give me an easy one to finish with."

He smiled.

"Earlier, I mentioned the mass consciousness that envelops the planet. It is this mass consciousness that affects our lives. Currently, the mass consciousness is burdened with negativity, and our lives are inevitably affected. Many of us will be exposed to deceit, suffering, crime, and so on. The planet itself provides the atmosphere for our experiences. Again, it is only experience. From a spiritual perspective, one experience is not better than another.

"We incarnate, knowing how negatively charged the atmosphere will be after we are born. We know what we are getting ourselves into. Every experience we encounter is agreed upon by our higher selves—our souls. I know how crazy that sounds, but that's the way it works.

"Before we are born, we carefully analyze the potential life that we will live. We have a basic framework of what the possibilities are, and we accept the risk. Once we are here, there are no accidents. Everything happens by agreement. How is this possible? Because the spiritual plane and the physical plane are interconnected. In many respects, the spiritual plane controls the physical plane.

Chapter 11 - Ogmios

"For instance, our higher selves and our guides are on the spiritual plane. These spirits contact us through our subconscious and consciousness. None of us are alone. We each have extraordinary help from Spirit on the physical plane. We each get what we need.

"We each incarnate with a plan and a life goal to learn certain lessons. This is what reincarnation is all about. We come to learn. I know that sounds crazy to many, but it only sounds crazy within the prevalent belief system."

Ogmios smiled and pressed the stop button on the recorder. "That was very good. This is a good start. Important people who have never heard any New Age concepts will hear this. The power brokers want to know what I'm up to, and any information that involves me is considered valuable. They want all that they can get their hands on.

"That's what these tapes are about. I'm trying to help them understand where the world is headed. I could do it face to face, but this is much better. We both know how hard it is to explain these concepts. That's why I'm using you — a New Age teacher."

He paused and looked at me, and I waited for another surprise.

"This isn't over?" I asked.

"No, I need to ask a favor."

I was apprehensive, and didn't reply.

He reached into his pocket and pushed an envelope across the table. "It's money. I need you to purchase a digital video camera, a tripod, and several high-density thumb drives."

"Why?" I asked.

"I want you to videotape your lectures at your school and send them to the address in the envelope. Send one per month for the next six months. That should be enough, and then you will be done and free."

I nodded. "Sure, I'll do that for you." We had already discussed how he was influencing the U.S. government, so I ventured a guess. "I take it, the videos are going to the U.S. government?"

Ogmios nodded. "Indeed."

"So, that's it? We're done?"

"One last thing," he said smiling. "Purchase a Sony; they are the best. And place the tripod close to where you are speaking, so that the voice quality is acceptable."

I smiled. "Sure." I could tell that he was a detail-oriented leader.

We arose and shook hands. I really felt like hugging him, but I held back, as I was unsure about his cultural and personal boundaries.

Shortly after the government meeting, I was given a meal and taken back to the airport for the trip back to Los Angeles. They asked if I wanted to spend the night, but I requested an immediate return. I planned on sleeping on the plane during the flight home.

I arrived back in Los Angeles shortly before sunrise, and Julie was already getting ready for work. She greeted me at the door and we hugged tightly, in silence. I could tell that she had been worried about me and was glad I was home.

I let out a long sigh of relief, and I promised her that our lives were finally going to calm down. I even believed it myself.

Chapter Twelve

Finding Your Soul

I arrived early for our next scheduled class and set up the new video camera. As Ogmios had recommended, I placed it close to the front, in the middle aisle. It was pointed directly at the large television screen, which was installed in the middle of the front wall. I was planning to use the screen with my laptop computer that night. The video was framed so that it would include me, standing next to the large screen.

By six o'clock, the class was almost full, with nearly one hundred people. Jim was not there for the class, and I was on my own, but that was not uncommon. We covered for each other when one of us had to travel, or could not attend due to some unforeseen issue.

I turned on the video camera, and then walked to the front of the class.

"Hello, everyone. Welcome to enlightenment school, and thank you for coming. My name is John Randall, and I will be speaking to you tonight. The topic is finding your soul, which is my favorite lecture and what I consider to be the foundation of this school. Many of you have heard the lecture before, but it is always good as a refresher.

"In the second hour, after a ten-minute break, we are going to have a group discussion about the topic.

"Because this is a long lecture, I would prefer that you ask your questions after I am finished. This is a PowerPoint presentation, and I will be using the big screen. Also, tonight I am recording the lecture on video. I will turn off the video camera once I am finished with the presentation and prior to your questions.

"I would also like to mention that I will be presenting my truths here, which I have assimilated over the past twenty plus years. The New Age movement is not about preaching dogma, or any ideas that you absolutely *have to* accept. Each person is free to accept or reject any information that is offered here, as we each have to ultimately find our own truths that we can accept and follow. In fact, it is my hope that each of you come to your own beliefs, in your own manner. Okay, let me begin with an introduction before I start the slides.

"<u>Finding your soul is a natural process.</u> In fact, there is nothing to do ... only to be. You do not have to proactively pursue religious or spiritual knowledge, or pursue some form of salvation. The truth is that all you need to do is live your life and you will evolve.

"The reason why is that your soul and your ego are entwined. You can try to live completely from your ego, but your soul will always find a way to exert some influence.

"This is why you don't have to look for your soul to find it. The fact is, everyone has a spark of light that is expanding. This spark of light is our soul and it has an agenda of its own. Eventually, our spark of light, our soul, will become more and more apparent. This will happen without any effort on our part, although not necessarily in this lifetime.

"<u>Everyone is on their own journey,</u> and will pursue spirituality in their own time and manner. This is a long journey of many lifetimes. And everyone's journey has the same goal: finding our

Chapter Twelve - Finding Your Soul

soul. Quite often, we are not even aware that is our goal. In fact, most people have no clue that is their ultimate goal.

"<u>Everyone will eventually find their soul.</u> This is guaranteed because of our spark of light that is constantly expanding. The soul does not regress. It either stays stagnant or expands. The soul expands at a faster rate when you feed it. Conversely, when we feed the ego, we slow our rate of growth. However, there is no right way to find the soul. Eventually we *all* find it.

"One question I always get is, 'How will I know if I have found my soul?' The answer is when you no longer feel alone. Meaning that you will feel a tangible connection with your soul, which will exist as a separate entity and as a part of your consciousness. Of course, this entity isn't separate, but it will feel that way. More importantly, it will feel real and it will seem to be a powerful companion. Once you are aware of this companion, you will have found your soul.

"While finding your soul is a natural process that everyone is doing, you can use a proactive approach to finding your soul. This is for those who have a longing desire to search for a deeper meaning to life. Your motive may have nothing to do with a search for your soul, but that is where it eventually leads. For all searchers, at some point there is an awakening.

"This awakening is about knowing. It is not about faith. When you find your soul, you know you have found it. There is no 'maybe' or 'possibly.' You know. And that process is about awakening.

"To find your soul, you have to do the work. When you go on a spiritual quest to find answers that you yearn to understand, it takes effort and persistence. Part of this lecture is to give you insight into that work, and what it can require to have an awakening.

"<u>You have to marginalize the ego.</u> My personal experience, on a twenty year spiritual quest, is that the ego has to be marginalized in order to expose the soul. Unless you marginalize the ego, the soul is submerged and the ego takes center stage.

"Most of you know the definition of marginalize, but I will repeat it for those who are unsure. To marginalize is to reduce something in a proactive manner. For instance, to marginalize smoking in restaurants, we made it illegal. To marginalize your ego, you need to institute proactive behaviors to reduce its influence.

"A proactive approach is accomplished with a spiritual path. This requires a new lifestyle, a lifestyle of spirituality. As you will see today, this is not something that is periodic, and it must be done on a constant basis: minute by minute, second by second. You have to live your quest to finding your soul.

"Okay, let's start the slides."

I pushed my remote control, and the first slide appeared on the screen.

What is the Ego?

- The ego is not our true self
- The ego is not our soul
- The ego is hiding the soul

"The ego is our temporary personality. It is our mask; it is our role. It is the illusion we have chosen to use for the pursuit of finding our soul. Most people like their ego personality and perceive it to be who they truly are. The very thought of their ego being an illusion is unsettling. That alone prevents most people from pursuing a spiritual path.

"Before you can find the soul, you have to understand the ego. This ego personality is an illusion and is 'caught in the bubble' of

Chapter Twelve - Finding Your Soul

this world and believes it is real. This is, perhaps, the hardest and most important thing to understand in order to find your soul.

"The ego personality is not real. In other words, the person you see up here tonight is not actually the real me. It's just a personality that I have assumed, so that I can learn lessons and help my soul to evolve. Don't lose sight of that fact.

"We don't want to be attached to our ego identities. However, this is very difficult to avoid, because the ego convinces us that it is real. When someone verbally attacks us, we tend to feel emotionally abused and identify with our ego identity. We not only feel vulnerable, but we distance ourselves from our souls.

"This is especially difficult in relationships. Our intimate others want us to fall in love with their ego identity and treat that identity as real. When you don't treat it as real, they get very upset."

The audience laughed, and I smiled.

"The ego personality is who we think we are—until we find the soul. Until that time, we think that we are real. We think that, when we took our first breath, our life was created as new. However, the only thing that was new was the creation of the ego. Hiding in the background was the soul, which was always there. The ego is a temporary creation, whereas the soul is eternal.

"The soul is much, much more than the temporary ego. The soul is the true self—the everlasting, eternal self. From the soul's perspective, this world that we live in is nothing more than an illusion—also called *maya* by the Eastern religions. This world we see is not real, and neither is the ego.

"Incredibly, most people have no knowledge that the ego is hiding the soul. The reason why is because they believe that the ego is real, and consequently they live in the ego and by the ego. The only way to see the ego for what it truly is, is to expose it for its narcissistic and hedonistic qualities.

"The ego is hiding your soul. The ego and the soul are entwined. However, until the soul is exposed by marginalizing the ego, the soul is submerged and hidden. To marginalize your ego, you need to take proactive steps to reduce its influence. Tonight, I will be talking extensively about many of these proactive behaviors that you can use."

I clicked the remote, and the next slide appeared.

How Do We Identify the Ego?

- The ego is your chattering mind
    - Temptation, Frustration, Fear, Anger, Worry
- The ego can never be satisfied.
- To expose the ego, ask these questions:
    - Is this the voice of the ego?
    - Is there any space?
    - Are you outside your mind?

"How do we identify the Ego? It's really pretty easy. The ego is your chattering mind. It is the voice in your head. Thoughts and feelings of the past, future, temptations, frustrations, fear, anger, and worry all originate in the ego. All of these are examples of the voice of the ego.

"Our thoughts and feelings are literally our ego keeping us trapped, keeping us away from our soul. Our ego does not care about our well being. It is only concerned with its existence.

"By being aware of these thoughts and feelings, you can create space when they arise. For instance, the next time you become angry, instead of completely identifying with the anger, step back and create space—thereby allowing spirit into your awareness. Become detached. You can then realize that you are not the anger, and that the anger is coming from the ego.

Chapter Twelve - Finding Your Soul

"You can do the same thing with fear or temptations. Just step back and see that it is not you, but your ego. By doing this, you expose the ego. In fact, by doing this, you literally gain control of the ego.

"Life is a daily contest between the ego and the soul, and someone is going to win. If the ego wins, this leads to stress, a busy mind, lost goals, lost serenity, lost contentment, and so on. If the soul wins, then you will live with serenity, contentment, and extreme satisfaction, which can also be called *joy*."

I paused and scanned the room. Everyone was in rapt attention.

"The Ego can never be satisfied. It is like an addiction, always waiting for an opportunity to gain control.

"Here is, perhaps, the most important thing you will learn tonight: the ego cannot exist in the present moment—in the moment when you are truly present, in the silence of a quiet mind. Why? Because the ego exists in the chattering mind. It is the soul that exists in the silence of the present moment.

"Thus, the key to exposing the ego is recognizing your chattering mind. When your mind is active, that is the ego. A busy mind is not the place to be, because it leads you away from your soul.

"Here are a few questions to ask yourself on a daily basis to expose your ego.

"One. 'Is this the voice of the Ego?' On the next slide, I will give you examples of the voice of the ego.

"Two. 'Is this for the higher good?' The ego does not aspire to help humanity. You can use this understanding to further marginalize the ego and live for a higher purpose.

"Negative thoughts or negative actions are always from the ego and will pull you down. Monitor your thoughts and do not let the ego disrupt your serenity and contentment. Remember, if you are living negatively, it will impact your life. Actions have consequences, and so do thoughts. Be vigilant, and be aware of those consequences. Don't let the ego pull you down.

"Three. 'Are you outside of your mind?' In this presentation, I define mind as your brain. The ego is in your head and the soul is in your heart. The soul exists as part of our consciousness, outside of the mind. The point here is to stand back from your thoughts and allow spirit to *also* be present. Make sure your spirit is *always* present, so that the ego does not dominate your thoughts.

"One thing I have learned is that you can't get to the root of fear unless you create space and get out of your mind. You have to let spirit into the conversation. Once spirit is acknowledged, then you can pop the bubble of fear. You can see through it, and recognize that you are creating it. You can literally see that the fear is being created by the ego.

"You can then tell your body to stop thinking and to go into the silence, thereby creating space. You control your body, not your ego. You have power over your ego, and you can tell it what to do. You can tell your body to connect to the quietness, to the silence, and it will obey.

"Let's do it right now. Everyone, close your eyes and breathe deeply. As you breathe, feel your breath and only listen to your breathing. Continue breathing, and silence your mind. Only listen to your breath. Let's do this for a few seconds. Keep listening to your breath and silence your mind. Now, place your consciousness on your fingers and feel them, keeping your eyes closed. Now, move your consciousness from finger to finger, feeling each one individually."

I paused to let them feel their fingers.

"As you are feeling your fingers, what are you thinking? Nothing! Your mind is silent. Why? Because the soul is more powerful than the ego. When you are connected to your soul, the mind is held at bay.

"Congratulations, you have just learned how to create space and keep your ego at bay. Also, you have just found your soul. The silence is literally the gateway to your soul."

I clicked the remote, and the next slide appeared.

The 7 Deadly Sins

1) Envy: Jealousy.
2) Gluttony: Having too much of something that you don't need.
3) Greed: Wanting more of something that you don't need.
4) Lust: Wanting some form of pleasure.
5) Pride: Identifying with your ego.
6) Sloth: Laziness.
7) Wrath: Anger.

"When I began my battle with the ego, I realized that I was feeding it. I was literally giving my power away by constantly feeding the ego. I was doing things that were not congruent with my spiritual values. So I started writing down those things I was doing which I wanted to stop. The first thing that stood out was the seven deadly sins.

"I think the seven deadly sins are a signpost for where we are at spiritually. They are, perhaps, the best tools that we can use to gauge our progress. A testament to this fact is that, once we attain spiritual enlightenment, these sins are no longer in our lives. So understanding what they are, and how they are holding us back from spiritual enlightenment, is important.

"The seven deadly sins are deadly. In the extreme, they lead to physical death. They represent addictions. If you want to ascend, then you have to overcome them. If you want to get closer to enlightenment, then you have to reduce them from your life. If you want to live to see the new world that is about to emerge, then you have to understand them.

"These are not really sins, in the sense that they are right or wrong. For most of us, they are simply milestones that reflect our advancement on our journey to enlightenment.

"As you become closer to God and closer to the wisdom that we are one with God, these so-called sins will vanish from your lives. This won't happen overnight; it takes time and spiritual work. If fact, it takes many lifetimes.

"Let's look a little closer at each of these.

"Envy: wanting something that someone else has because of jealousy. Do you want a nicer house, a nicer car—or perhaps a nicer spouse?"

The class laughed, and I smiled.

"All of these envious thoughts run counter to the spiritual concept of contentment and gratefulness. Like all of the seven deadly sins, envy causes you to identify with your ego and thereby hides you soul. The soul is in the background, being ignored, and the ego is in charge. That is what happens when one of these sins is active. We literally push God to the side and live by our will, and we do this by using our egos.

"Gluttony: having too much of something that you don't need. Food and TV are the big two in our culture; alcohol is another. The solution is living simply, so you can limit extravagance.

"Greed: wanting more of something that you don't need. Gluttony and greed are very similar. They are both hedonistic impulses that are ego driven. Instead of identifying with the soul, we identify with the ego and what the ego wants. This leads to selfish behavior, that is counterproductive in the spiritual sense. Once you begin working on your spirituality, these hedonistic

Chapter Twelve - Finding Your Soul

impulses are curtailed. Eventually they go away, and we begin to live an ascetic, pure life.

"My favorite greed anecdote is from the movie *Wall Street*, when Darian is getting out of the ocean. She looks up at Gordon Gecko's mansion and says, 'If I could have this, it would *almost* be enough.' Her one thought had greed, envy, gluttony, lust, envy, and pride—all at once.

"Lust: wanting some form of mental stimulation. Some form of pleasure. Most people think of lust as sexual desire. However, this can be anything that gives you pleasure, such as food or a drug. Any physical addiction falls into this category.

"Addictions can be truly debilitating, because they come from the ego and allow our egos to control us. As a spiritual being, our mission is to slay the ego and identify with the soul. Addictions have the power to keep us firmly rooted in our egos, so they must be removed from our lives.

"One of the things I started doing when I began my spiritual journey in 1989 was to eliminate my addictions. It is amazing how many things you can remove from your life, in order to get closer to your soul. They are easy to identify. Try to live one day without the ego telling you what to do, or what to put in your body. For instance, try not to put anything in your body that is not healthy. Or, try not to think a single thought that is not for the highest good. These are just two examples of how lust can control our lives.

"I ordered these in alphabetical order, but pride should really go last. It encompasses all of the other sins, and truly represents all of them combined. Pride is identifying with your ego.

"Pride is the most difficult sin to overcome. How many of you knew that identifying with this world and your ego identity is a sin? How many of you know that this world is an illusion and isn't real? The ego identity, which you perceive as real, is also an illusion. There are parts of your soul that come through, but there are many aspects of your personality that simply come from your ego.

"The world that we live in is an illusion. The more you identify with it, the more you are caught in the bubble. Once you begin your spiritual journey, you will pop this bubble and see it for what it is. Then you will begin to identify with your soul and see the perfection of life, and that the world is divinely ordered.

"Sloth is lacking discipline, lacking responsibility, laziness, and not being motivated. Once you begin your spiritual path, you come to understand that we are here to accomplish something. We are here to learn lessons. Life is not about hedonism, although we can enjoy it. Life is about growth, spiritual growth. And to attain that growth, we can't just sit in front of a television every day. You have to be motivated and stick to your path. If you don't know what that path is, you should be motivated to find it.

"Wrath is what I like to call pride on steroids. It encompasses anger, not being gentle, not accommodating, not comforting, and not caring. Wrath is the telltale sign that the ego is definitely in charge. If you get upset, that is your way of telling God that you are not content or grateful. You are saying, 'God, I am not happy with the life you have given me. God, I do not love you. *God*, I am so mad at you!'"

Several people laughed.

"Old souls tend to be kind and gentle. That is how you can tell whether they are old souls. You become gentle when you begin to recognize that you're an eternal being, who is not only loved by God, but is literally one with God, and one with humanity. When you get close to enlightenment, you begin to recognize that by getting upset or angry at another, you are identifying with your ego.

Chapter Twelve - Finding Your Soul

"By creating space, you can literally have one foot in this world and one foot in spirit. You can then stand back from anger and release it. The anger can start to rise, and you can nip it quite easily—if you have that one foot in spirit. Moreover, if you can identify the ego through your chattering mind, you can see that *that* is not you. Not the *real* you."

I clicked the remote, and the next slide appeared.

Feeding the Ego

- Ungratefulness
- Selfishness
- Arrogance
- Past/Future: Chattering Mind
- Fear

"In addition to the seven deadly sins, I have found five other behaviors that feed the ego. Most of these, I have already mentioned. But I will go over them again.

"Ungratefulness is lacking contentment, not being happy, and not being satisfied. This is an unnatural state, created by negative emotions which come from the ego. As an eternal soul, there is no reason *not* to be grateful. What is the gift of life worth?

"Selfishness: caring more about yourself than humanity. This is where society has driven us. At my last job, the company pushed me to be a high achiever, which was rewarded. They thought this was good business, but it instilled a sense of individuality and selfishness. This is no different than most businesses today.

"Eventually, we come to learn that life is about service to humanity, and not self service to one's self interest. Corporations do not care about humanity. They care about the bottom line. They care about their self interest. Selfishness is ingrained into us when we first enter school, are given grades and are forced to compete against one another. This mentality is carried forward into the business world. What no one recognizes is that, by being selfish, we are feeding our egos and not feeding our souls.

"Arrogance: Feeling superior to others or above the law. Arrogance often leads to being mean or willful, dishonesty, stealing, or addictions. This goes hand in hand with pride and identifying with the ego.

"These negative behaviors eventually expose the ego for what it truly is—a mask that only cares about its own survival. Do we serve humanity or self? This is the question we eventually come to ask, although perhaps not in this lifetime.

"The Chattering Mind is where the ego lives. We feed our egos constantly with our chattering mind. For most people, it is an ongoing process that never ceases.

"Fear: Lacking trust in God or trust in Creator's eternal grace. After lust, fear is the ego's favorite weapon to get our attention. Fear is created in our mind by our ego. If we have trust in our eternal destiny, there is no reason to fear. If you can truly see that this world is an illusion and the soul is indestructible and cannot be damaged, then trust becomes possible.

"The ego uses fear to keep us trapped in the illusion of life. This will become apparent, if you attempt to marginalize the ego. Note that fear is a strong emotion and that the ego uses these emotions to control us. The key to getting out of these traps is to silence the mind."

"Okay, let's take a ten minute break. That is a lot of information to absorb."

* * * * *

I paused the video camera.

Most of the class walked outside and were likely making new friends.

Chapter Twelve - Finding Your Soul

Jim had just arrived, and headed towards me to say hello. We chatted for a few minutes about our activities of the day.

"Tell me more about Ogmios," Jim said. "That must have been cool talking to him."

I smiled. "Yeah, it was a kick. I think he actually believes in the New Age movement. He wouldn't say it, or say that he had metaphysical beliefs, but he seemed to be a believer."

"And these videos we're making are going directly to him and the Washington power brokers?"

"I think so."

"Wow, that's amazing."

We were both silent, considering the possibilities.

"Okay, let's get the class going again," I said.

"I'll bring everyone in," Jim said.

After everyone had returned to their seats, I clicked the remote, and the next slide appeared.

Love & Trust

- Love yourself with purity and respect.
- Love others with compassion and gentleness.
- Love God with honor and truth.

- Trust that your life was pre-planned.
- Trust that life is divinely ordered.
- Trust that nothing can happen to you that is not supposed to.

"Love yourself with purity and respect. This is why it is important to marginalize your ego. The ego will constantly make it difficult for you to love yourself. The reason for this is that, if you truly love yourself, you will live a pure lifestyle. And the ego does not want to live a pure lifestyle. The ego wants to wallow in the seven deadly sins and feed itself with sensory experiences that make this life seem real.

"Love others with compassion and gentleness. Don't take affronts personally, and forgive another person's lack of spiritual awareness. Be compassionate and sensitive towards the plight of others, even when someone's ego is running wild. Not because you agree with their choices, but in spite of them. Everyone is on a spiritual path, so *always* respect the paths of others. The recommendation to not judge others is true wisdom.

"Love God, the Creator, with honor and truth. Be true to yourself and you will be true to God. This can only be achieved by marginalizing the ego and feeding the soul, and you must know yourself in order to be true to yourself.

"In addition to these simple directives about love, please consider these three statements about trust:

"Trust that your life was pre-planned. Everything that happens has already happened. Before we incarnate, we carefully select a life that can teach us the lessons we need to learn. This selection is done through a planning process that analyzes future lifetimes. It is a highly complex process where many souls plan and incarnate together. The reason it comes off so smoothly, is that everything has already happened. Life, in many ways, is simply playback or rewind. All events have already happened and are already contained within the imagination of God.

"Trust that life is divinely ordered. This is why there are no accidents. God is running the show. We can think we have free will, but God is making sure that life is going according to plan. We do have a degree of free choice, and can choose how we are going to live our day. But, on most days when we wake up, our day has already been determined. Not because God is going to dictate what we choose, but because our beliefs are known to God, who can anticipate what we will choose. You see, it is our beliefs that dictate our behaviors. And it is our collective beliefs that dictate society's behavior.

"Trust that nothing can happen to you that is not supposed to happen. This goes back to my previous comment. Our beliefs create our reality, and we create everything that happens in our life. Not one thing can happen that was not created by our beliefs. This seems impossible, but it is so. This is why we eventually come to learn, over many lifetimes, that the ego is causing all of our dysfunctions and disharmony. At some point, we come to learn that we either feed the ego or feed the soul.

"What is amazing is that the ego is so good at camouflaging its motives that many of you do not even believe my three statements about trust. The ego is a master of evoking doubt. After all, it is the ego's existence that is at stake. For, once you come to understand the ego and stop feeding it, it fades away."

I clicked the remote, and the next slide appeared.

Finding Your Soul

- The past, future: chattering mind.
- The present moment.
- Rooted in being.

"So, to review some of what we have already discussed....

"Doing battle with the ego and learning how *not* to feed it is a good practice, but what you really need is a spiritual path. In a previous class, we talked about using tools like astrology and numerology for self discovery, and a summary of those class notes is available on the back table.

"The starting point of your spiritual path is understanding yourself and your ego. And from that understanding, relegating the ego to a limited role in your life.

"Because the ego requires thought, I call the ego the *chattering mind*. It is your job, once you begin a spiritual path, to silence this chattering mind. The quieter you keep the mind, the more clearly you can feel and hear your soul and avoid fears and temptations that poison the mind.

"We talked about how your soul can be found in the present moment — in the silence — and this is where you want to spend your time. When your mind is silent, the ego is marginalized.

"The silence provides the gateway to the soul. It is literally the channel where you connect to your spirit. This is why we meditate and do yoga. We need to get out of our minds and connect to our souls.

"Knowing this silence, you can have one foot connected to your spirit at all times. Even if the ego is chattering, you can stand back and create enough space so that you can perceive your spirit. This is how you become grounded in the present. You quiet the mind and then keep it quiet.

"Another way to silence the mind is to feel your breath, and you can practice that exercise at home. This is why meditating and yoga are such spiritual endeavors and should be part of your spiritual journey. Once your mind is silent, you can think with your heart and not with your chattering mind. You can think with your heart — your feelings — and you can trust them. If you follow your heart, it will always lead you where you need to go.

"Space is just another way of being present and connected to the soul. Creating space between your chattering mind and your soul's perception is how you stay rooted in being.

"Let's say you are worried. In that moment, the ego is forcing you to feel fear by using thought. Without thought, you cannot feel fear. If you stand back, away from your body, and perceive that your soul is watching from across the room, then you can silence your thoughts and subsequently the fear.

Chapter Twelve – Finding Your Soul

"When you are afraid—and all you can think about is your fear, stop and create space. Know that your fear is coming from your mind, your ego. Step away from it. Then go into the space—into the silence—and find comfort in the present moment. This is how you find relief from your chattering mind to overcome fear.

"For instance, if you are in a bank and it is suddenly stormed by robbers, how do you react? Most likely, your mind will race with fear. However, you can stand back from the situation and feel completely safe. This is the same thing as what I call 'rooted in being.' Instead of giving the robbery your attention, you can detach from the situation. You can literally go out of your mind, so that if someone calls your name, you will not hear them. This is also what I call having one foot in this world and one foot in the spirit world.

"Rooted in being is when the ego is held at bay and the mind has been silenced. Then we can connect to the soul. Over time, as you practice entering the silence and connecting to your soul on a regular basis, it becomes much easier to remain rooted in being, even when you are not meditating."

I clicked the remote, and the next slide appeared.

A Spiritual Path

- We are here to grow and develop mastery over the ego.
- Our spiritual path is accomplished in two parts: not feeding the ego, and feeding the soul.
- Every morning is a new day, a new opportunity to feed the soul.

"After you have found your soul, it is time to focus on your spiritual path, which could also be called a spiritual journey. We are here to grow, to vibrate higher, and to develop mastery over the ego. Mastery over the ego leads to enlightenment, and a complete recognition that we are one with God.

"For some of us, our spiritual path is a profound experience that we take very seriously. Other people only dabble in it, and prefer to live lives that are more firmly grounded in the ego. Both approaches are quite acceptable to God. Everyone has their own journey and can choose the path that they wish to follow.

"All paths lead to the same destination: enlightenment. My point is that, even if you are completely oblivious to a spiritual path, your life is still focused on developing mastery. It may not appear that way, but everyone is making strides towards spiritual enlightenment.

"Enlightenment is obtained by accomplishing three smaller goals:

- Finding purity by avoiding the seven daily sins and other destructive behaviors.
- Becoming rooted in being by constantly feeling your connection to spirit, and remaining aware of the ego or chattering mind.
- Making spiritual growth your top priority and always striving to learn more.

"Our spiritual path is accomplished in two parts. Part one is not feeding the ego, and is, by far, the most difficult. The second part is feeding the soul. Note that you can feed the soul as much as you want by meditating, reading spiritual material, going to seminars, doing yoga, et cetera. However, unless the ego is marginalized, your spiritual path will be impeded by your ego.

"It is my opinion that, by not feeding the ego, we automatically feed the soul. Simply by ignoring the ego, we open a connection to our soul for guidance. Moreover, by focusing on our life's goal, we feed the soul. This is another way of feeding the soul. Find out

Chapter Twelve - Finding Your Soul

what you need to do in this lifetime and then do it. Follow your heart and go where you are led.

"Every morning is a new day, a new chance to live with love and trust, and thereby feed the soul. These are the two most important things for a spiritual path: love and trust. Love God enough to be grateful for your eternal life. Love others. Trust that nothing can happen to you that is not for your benefit. Be so bold as to accept and embrace whatever comes your way.

"Every day when you wake up, you should meditate or read a prayer that connects you to spirit. Every morning, I read my Morning Checklist, which I consider a daily prayer. I attempt to create a connection to Spirit first thing in the morning, and then I try to hold it for the rest of the day. This works. I find myself constantly remembering that my spirit is with me and that my ego is vying for my attention."

I clicked the remote, and the next slide appeared.

Morning Checklist

1) Acknowledge the perfection. Everything is divinely ordered.
2) Be grateful. Be humble.
3) Enjoy the ride. Life is a gift.
4) Live content. Not wanting.
5) Live pure. Without temptation.
6) Live simply. Without extravagance.
7) Stay healthy. Eat right and exercise.
8) Stay on the path. Achieve your life's purpose.
9) Use loving kindness. Be gentle.

"This simple checklist is self-explanatory. Note that my morning checklist is actually much larger and includes reminders about avoiding ways that I can feed my ego. It takes me a few minutes to read my list each morning, while I eat my cereal."

"That's it. Let's take a break, and then we can come back and talk about it. There is a printout of the presentation in the back."

I stopped my slide presentation, and turned off the video camera that was recording for Ogmios.

After the break, I answered a few questions, and then the class had a spirited group discussion. I let the class do most of the talking.

I was busy wondering who was going to be watching this instructional video back in Washington. Were the power brokers of the world really going to see this? If so, there was a good chance they would recognize the potential of these concepts for peace on Earth. They might actually begin to promote these ideas — if they truly wanted peace.

I hoped that it wasn't too idealistic to expect such an outcome. I hoped that our leaders were wise enough to recognize that it was possible for a person to find his soul. And that the more who found it, the better off humanity would be.

EPILOGUE

I am happy to say that the protest marches resisting the New Age movement died down within six months. Not that anybody was really speaking out against the protestors. But it seemed like the protestors eventually grew tired of fighting an enemy who never fought back. Violence against known New Age proponents had gradually diminished, too, ever since the government told the population that they did not pose a threat of any kind and that they were espousing peace.

And things were looking up in Europe. The AC could not gain control and neither side was gaining much ground. It was becoming a stalemate. Fighting around the world gradually began to cease, and it seemed like people were expecting peace talks to start in the near future. At least, that's what our TV news reports told us.

After my meeting with the Underground leader, I did not do much travelling, despite the fact that it was becoming safer to venture forth. As social unrest eased, I also became less and less concerned about personal security issues.

The worst was apparently over. We had lived through a tumultuous time, but most of the commotion and trauma had disappeared from our lives. Julie and I were finally able to return to a relatively calm and serene life together. When Julie came home each night, I was there to greet her with a smile, and we rarely worried about the issues of the day anymore.

There were still some tumultuous earth changes from time to time. But overall, I began to feel much more hopeful and more at peace than I had ever felt. It was apparent that the new age was dawning.